Become a top fact-fetcher with CGP!

Quick question — have you memorised the facts in CGP's Knowledge Organiser for AQA GCSE Business?

You have? Great! Now you can use this Knowledge Retriever to check you've really got everything stuck in your brain.

There are memory tests for each topic, plus mixed quiz questions to make extra sure you've really remembered all the important bits. Enjoy!

CGP — still the best! ☺

Our sole aim here at CGP is to produce the highest quality books — carefully written, immaculately presented and dangerously close to being funny.

Then we work our socks off to get them out to you — at the cheapest possible prices.

Contents

How to Use This Book...................................2

Section 1 — Business in the Real World

Why Businesses Exist......................................3
Enterprise and Entrepreneurs.......................5
Business Ownership Structures.....................7
More Business Ownership Structures..........9
Mixed Practice Quizzes................................11
Business Aims and Objectives.....................13
More on Business Objectives......................15
Stakeholders..17
Resources...19
Mixed Practice Quizzes................................21
Revenue, Costs and Profit...........................23
The Business Plan.......................................25
Location...27
Mixed Practice Quizzes................................29
Expanding Businesses.................................31
Internal Expansion......................................33
External Expansion.....................................35
Mixed Practice Quizzes................................37

Section 2 — Influences on Business

Businesses and the Law...............................39
Technology and Business............................41
Ethical Considerations.................................43
Environmental Influences............................45
Mixed Practice Quizzes................................47

Businesses and the Economic Climate.......49
Competition..51
Globalisation and Exchange Rates..............53
Risks in Business...55
Mixed Practice Quizzes................................57

Section 3 — Business Operations

Supply Chains..59
More on Supply Chains...............................61
Production and Efficiency...........................63
Mixed Practice Quizzes................................65
Quality...67
Quality Management...................................69
Customer Service..71
More on Customer Service.........................73
Mixed Practice Quizzes................................75

Section 4 — Human Resources

Internal Organisational Structures..............77
More on Organisational Structures............79
Contracts of Employment...........................81
Mixed Practice Quizzes................................83
Recruitment...85
Staff Training..87
Financial Motivation....................................89
Non-Financial Motivation............................91
Mixed Practice Quizzes................................93

Section 5 — Marketing

The Marketing Mix 95
Market Research 97
More on Market Research 99
Product Life Cycles 101
Extension Strategies 103
Mixed Practice Quizzes 105
Product Portfolios 107
Product Development 109
Price 111
Pricing Strategies 113
Mixed Practice Quizzes 115
Methods of Promotion 117
More Methods of Promotion 119
Place 121
E-Commerce 123
Mixed Practice Quizzes 125

Section 6 — Finance

Sources of Finance 127
More Sources of Finance 129
Investments 131
Mixed Practice Quizzes 133
Break-Even Analysis 135
More on Break-Even Analysis 137
Cash Flow 139
More on Cash Flow 141
Mixed Practice Quizzes 143
Income Statements 145
Profit Margins 147
Statements of Financial Position 149
More on Statements of
  Financial Position 151
Analysis of Financial Statements 153
Mixed Practice Quizzes 155

Answers 157

Published by CGP.
Based on the classic CGP style created by Richard Parsons.

Editors: Molly Barker, Liam Dyer, Katherine Faudemer and Jack Simm.
Contributor: Colin Harber-Stuart

With thanks to Michael Bushell and Sarah Pattison for the proofreading.
With thanks to Hannah Wilkie for the copyright research.

ISBN: 978 1 83774 015 4

Printed by Elanders Ltd, Newcastle upon Tyne.
Clipart from Corel®

Text, design, layout and original illustrations © Coordination Group Publications Ltd (CGP) 2024
All rights reserved.

Photocopying this book is not permitted, even if you have a CLA licence.
Extra copies are available from CGP with next day delivery. • 0800 1712 712 • www.cgpbooks.co.uk

How to Use This Book

Every page in this book has a matching page in the GCSE Business **Knowledge Organiser**. Before using this book, try to **memorise** everything on a Knowledge Organiser page. Then follow these **seven steps** to see how much knowledge you're able to retrieve...

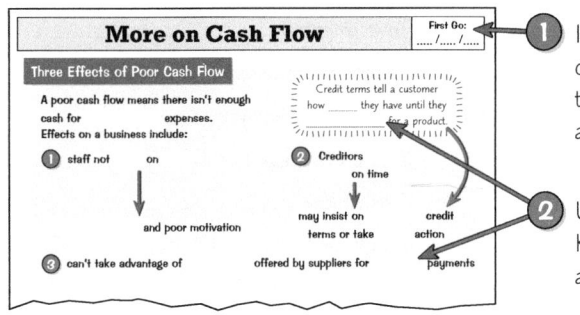

(1) In this book, there are two versions of each page. Find the **'First Go'** of the page you've tried to memorise, and write the **date** at the top.

(2) Use what you've learned from the Knowledge Organiser to **fill in** any dotted lines or white spaces.

(3) Use the Knowledge Organiser to **check your work**.
Use a **different colour pen** to write in anything you missed or that wasn't quite right. This lets you see clearly what you **know** and what you **don't know**.

(4) After doing the First Go page, **wait a few days**. This is important because **spacing out** your retrieval practice helps you to remember things better.

(5) Now do the **Second Go** page.
The Second Go page is harder — it has more things missing.

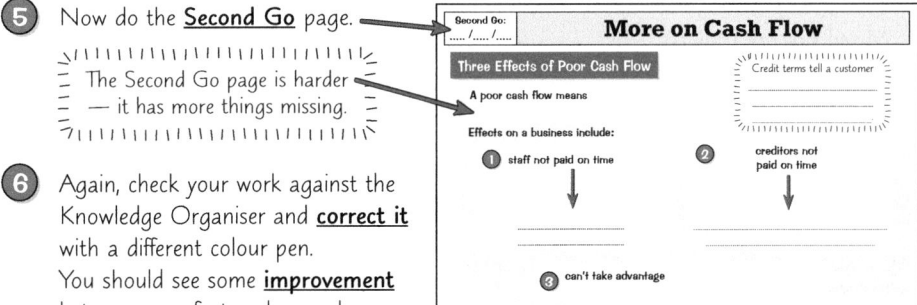

(6) Again, check your work against the Knowledge Organiser and **correct it** with a different colour pen.
You should see some **improvement** between your first and second go.

(7) **Wait** another few days, then try to reproduce any facts, formulas, tables or diagrams from the Knowledge Organiser page on a **blank piece of paper**. You can also have a go at any **example questions**. If you can do this, you'll know you've **really learned it**.

There are also **Mixed Practice Quizzes** dotted throughout the book:
- The quizzes come in sets of four. They test a mix of content from the previous few pages.
- Do each quiz on a different day — write the date you do each one at the top of the quiz.
- Tick the questions you get right and record your score in the box at the end.
- Quiz questions marked with * have the answers given at the back of the book.

Section 1 — Business in the Real World

Why Businesses Exist

First Go: ...../...../.....

Purpose of Businesses

Businesses sell products to   .

Products can be   or   .

| GOOD | An ...., e.g. a chocolate bar or an e-book |
| SERVICE | An .... performed by other people to aid the customer, e.g. .... |

Needs vs Wants

Goods or services can be:

1. Needs — things you ....

2. Wants — things you'd .... to have but can ....

Five Reasons for Starting a Business

1. To produce   .

2. To provide a   .

3. To .... to other businesses or individual customers.

4. To fulfil a   .

5. To benefit   .

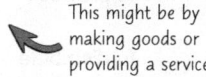 This might be by making goods or providing a service.

Three Sectors of the Economy

Sector of Economy	What it Does	Example of Business
1	.... raw materials for making goods or services. Raw materials can be: • extracted from the ground • .... •	• .... industry • .... industry • Fishing industry
2 SECONDARY	.... goods.	• .... • Construction industry
3 TERTIARY	Services can be for other .... or	• Advertising industry • .... • .... • .... • Banks

Second Go: ...../...../.....

Why Businesses Exist

Purpose of Businesses

Businesses sell
Products can be

	An ...., e.g.
SERVICE	e.g.

Needs vs Wants

Goods or services can be:

1. Needs —

2. Wants —

Five Reasons for Starting a Business

1.
2. To provide
3. To distribute
4. To fulfil
5.

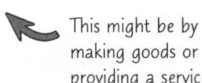
This might be by making goods or providing a service.

Three Sectors of the Economy

Sector of Economy	What it Does	Example of Business
1	Produces .... for making .... Raw materials can be: • • •	• • •
2 SECONDARY		• •
3	Provides .... Services can be	• • • •

Section 1 — Business in the Real World

Enterprise and Entrepreneurs

First Go: ..... / ..... / .....

Enterprise

ENTERPRISE — the process of identifying _____ and taking advantage of them.

> Enterprise can involve _____ or _____ an existing one.

Four Qualities of Entrepreneurs

ENTREPRENEUR — someone who takes on the _____ of _____.

An entrepreneur should be:

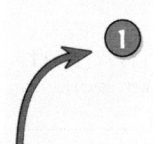

_____ hours and lots of _____ tasks (e.g. accounting, business planning, sales and marketing).

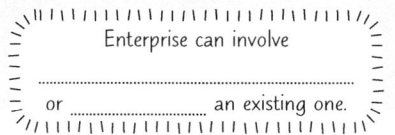

② To come up with ideas and _____ problems.

④ Willing to _____. Running a business involves _____. May need to give up current _____ and will need to _____.

③ Need to keep on top of _____ as well as _____ for the future.

Six Objectives of Entrepreneurs

Reasons why someone might decide to be an entrepreneur:

① Financial reasons
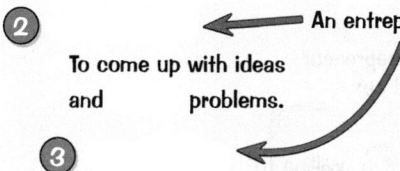
_____ business
↓
↓
earn more _____

② Gap in the market identified — _____ a good or service _____ provides.

③ Be their own boss — make own _____ about business.

④ _____ working hours — work around _____.

⑤ Following an interest in what they do ➡ _____ job

⑥ _____ with current job, _____ new business ➡ more _____

Section 1 — Business in the Real World

Enterprise and Entrepreneurs

Second Go: ...../...../.....

Enterprise

ENTERPRISE —

Enterprise can involve ....
or ....

Four Qualities of Entrepreneurs

ENTREPRENEUR —

An entrepreneur should be:

1. ....
   Long hours and

2. ....
   To come up

3. ....
   Need to

4. Willing to ....
   Running a business involves

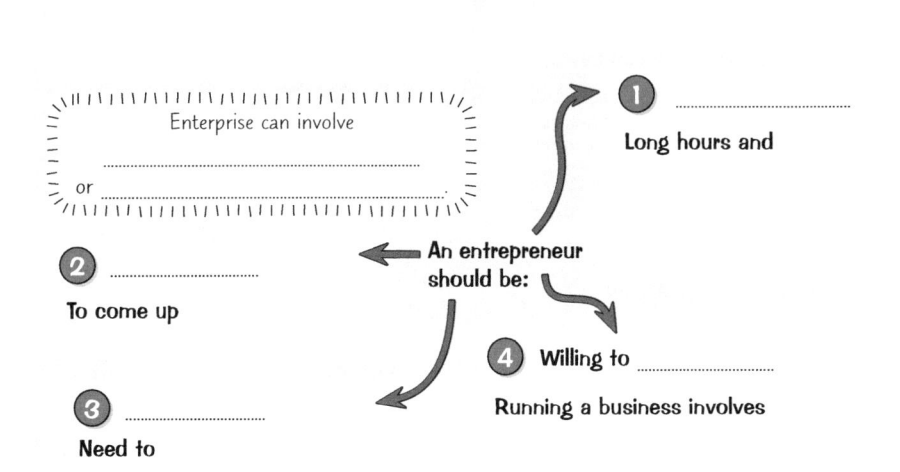

Six Objectives of Entrepreneurs

Reasons why someone might decide to be an entrepreneur:

1. Financial reasons

2. Gap in the market identified —

3. Be their own .... —

4. .... —

5. interested in what they do →

6. .... with current job

new business →

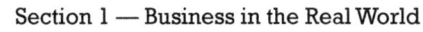

Section 1 — Business in the Real World

Business Ownership Structures

First Go: ..... / ..... / .....

Unlimited vs Limited Liability

UNLIMITED LIABILITY —

business owners are _____ for paying back _____ if the business _____ (even if they have to _____ everything they own).

LIMITED LIABILITY —

_____ is legally responsible for paying back _____, not the owners. They only risk losing the _____ they have _____.

Legal Identities

INCORPORATED —

the business has a separate _____ from its owners. Any money, property, bills, etc. belong to the _____ not the _____.

UNINCORPORATED —

the business has _____. Suing the business means suing the _____.

Sole Traders

SOLE TRADER — a business with just _____. (They can have other employees)

Most _____ businesses, e.g. plumbers, hairdressers.

Advantages
- easy to _____
- full control over _____ and _____

Disadvantages
- _____ liability
- unincorporated
- _____ responsibility can mean long _____ and few _____
- hard to _____

Partnerships

E.g. solicitors, doctors' surgeries.

PARTNERSHIP — a business owned by a _____. Partners usually have an equal _____ in the business and equal _____.

Advantages
- more owners means more...
- _____
- _____
- _____ (money)
- people to _____

Disadvantages
- _____ liability (usually)
- each partner is _____ for what all the others do
- partners have to share _____
- partners might disagree on _____

Section 1 — Business in the Real World

Business Ownership Structures

Second Go: ...../...../......

Unlimited vs Limited Liability

UNLIMITED LIABILITY —

LIMITED LIABILITY —

Legal Identities

INCORPORATED —

UNINCORPORATED —

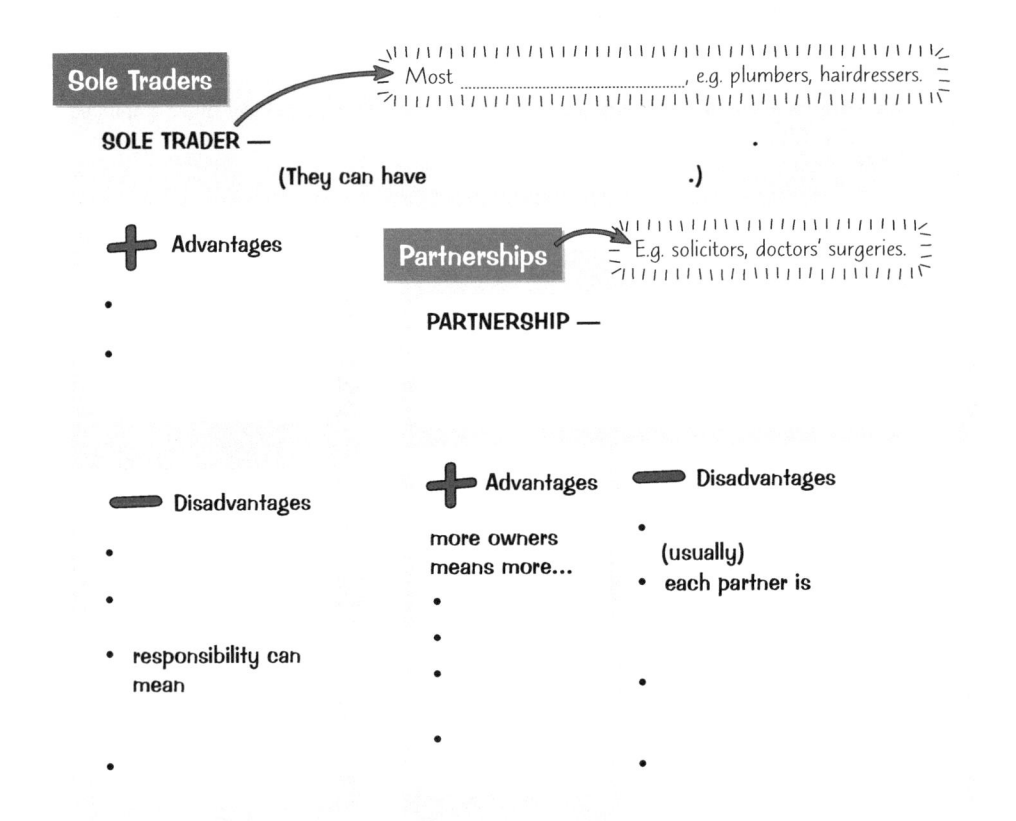

Sole Traders

Most ...., e.g. plumbers, hairdressers.

SOLE TRADER —

(They can have   .)

+ Advantages
-
-

Partnerships

E.g. solicitors, doctors' surgeries.

PARTNERSHIP —

+ Advantages

more owners means more...
-
-
-
-

— Disadvantages
- (usually)
- each partner is
-
-

— Disadvantages
-
-
- responsibility can mean
-

Section 1 — Business in the Real World

More Business Ownership Structures

First Go: ...../...../......

Private Limited Companies

Owned by _____ .
Shares can only be sold when _____
_____ .

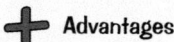 Advantages
- _____ liability
- incorporated
- easier to get _____

━━ Disadvantages
- expensive to _____
- required to _____
_____ every year

Public Limited Companies

Owned by _____ .
Company shares traded on _____
and can be bought and sold by _____ .

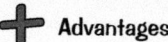 Advantages
- _____ liability
-
- more capital can be raised
- easy to _____ and _____

━━ Disadvantages
- lots of shareholders — hard to _____ ,
_____ and _____ between more people
- possible for _____ to buy enough shares to _____ the company
- accounts are _____ , so _____ can see if business is _____

Not-for-Profit Organisations

Don't try to make a profit:
- generate income to _____
_____

- surplus put back into the _____
or used for _____

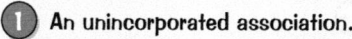 Advantages
- can have charitable status = _____
- can be eligible for _____

Can choose to be:

(1) An unincorporated association.
Easy to _____ but the people involved have _____ liability.

━━ Disadvantages
- can be hard to set up due to _____
- dependent on _____
and _____
- can be hard to _____
- may rely on _____

(2) Incorporated.
_____ liability for people involved.

Often 'limited by guarantee' — members agree to pay a _____ if the business goes _____ .

\\\
Social enterprises are a type of not-for-profit that make money selling products but use the profit to _____ .
///

Section 1 — Business in the Real World

Second Go: ..... / ..... / .....

More Business Ownership Structures

Private Limited Companies

Owned by ....
Shares can

➕ Advantages
-
-
-

➖ Disadvantages
-
-

Public Limited Companies

Owned by ....
Company shares

➕ Advantages
-
-
-
- easy to

➖ Disadvantages
- lots of

- possible for

- accounts are

Not-for-Profit Organisations

Don't try to
- generate

- surplus put

➕ Advantages
-
-

Can choose to be:

1) An .... association.
   Easy to

➖ Disadvantages
-
-
-
-

2)
Limited

Often 'limited by guarantee' —

.... are a type of not-for-profit that make money selling products but ....

Section 1 — Business in the Real World

Mixed Practice Quizzes

Here are some quick questions to test what you've learnt on p.3-10.
You are liable to mark each quiz yourself and tot up your own score.

Quiz 1 — Date: ...... / ...... / ......

1) List four disadvantages of operating as a not-for-profit organisation.
2) What is meant by 'limited liability'?
3) List four qualities an entrepreneur should have.
4) Outline the difference between a good and a service.
5) What are the three sectors of the economy?
6) Give four disadvantages of operating as a sole trader.
7) What is meant by the term 'limited by guarantee'?
8) Give one example of a business that operates as a partnership.
9) True or false? Expanding a business is an example of enterprise.
10) Who owns a public limited company?

Total:

Quiz 2 — Date: ...... / ...... / ......

1) Why can having lots of shareholders be a disadvantage for a public limited company?
2) Give three advantages of a private limited company as a business ownership model.
3) What is an entrepreneur?
4) What sector of the economy provides services?
5) True or false? A sole trader is a business with only one employee.
6) List six reasons why someone may become an entrepreneur.
7) What is the difference between needs and wants?
8) Give two advantages of being a not-for-profit organisation.
9) Which sector of the economy manufactures goods?
10) What does it mean if a business is incorporated?

Total:

Section 1 — Business in the Real World

Mixed Practice Quizzes

Quiz 3 Date: ...... / ...... / ......

1) Explain what social enterprises are.
2) List five reasons for starting a business.
3) Why should an entrepreneur be organised?
4) Give four disadvantages of a partnership as a business ownership model.
5) What sector of the economy does the mining industry belong to?
6) Give three disadvantages of operating as a public limited company.
7) Give two examples of a tertiary sector business.
8) What does it mean if a business is unincorporated?
9) Give one example of a business that usually operates as a sole trader.
10) What is meant by 'enterprise'?

Total:

Quiz 4 Date: ...... / ...... / ......

1) List four advantages of operating as a public limited company.
2) What is a sole trader?
3) What does the primary sector of the economy produce?
4) What actions may a not-for-profit organisation take if they have a surplus of income?
5) What is meant by 'unlimited liability'?
6) True or false? Having flexible working hours is a reason why someone may decide to be an entrepreneur.
7) Why should an entrepreneur be hardworking?
8) Outline the advantages of a partnership as a business ownership model.
9) Give two examples of a business in the secondary sector of the economy.
10) Give two disadvantages of a private limited company as a business ownership model.

Total:

Business Aims and Objectives

First Go: ..... / ..... / .....

Aims

AIM — an overall _____ that a business wants to _____ .

Once a firm _____ , it needs to _____ .

Seven Business Aims

1. _____ profit — this is an aim for _____ firms.

2. _____ — having enough money to _____ , e.g. to pay staff and buy _____ to sell.

3. Growth — could be increasing:
   - _____
   - products sold
   - _____ income

   Growth can be:
   - _____ (in the same country)
   - _____ (expand into other countries)

Objectives

1. act as _____ on the way to an _____

2. act as _____ for firms to _____

3. _____ can be used to _____ whether a firm has been _____ .

   E.g. _____ = growth
   _____ = _____ income from sales by 30% over two years.

4. Increase _____ — take sales from _____ or bring in _____ .

5. Do what's _____ — acting in ways that are best for _____ and are _____ .

6. Increase _____ — making shareholders more _____ by increasing the _____ of the firm.

7. Customer _____ — when customers are happy with the product. Can be measured by _____ .

Section 1 — Business in the Real World

Business Aims and Objectives

Second Go: ..... / ..... / .....

Aims

AIM —

Once a firm knows

Seven Business Aims

1. Maximise profit —

2.

3. Growth
   — could be increasing:
   -
   -
   -

   Growth can be:
   -
   -

Objectives

1. act as

2. act as

3. can be used to

   E.g. Aim =
   Objective =

4. Increase market share —

5. Do what's right —

6. Increase shareholder value —

7. Customer satisfaction —

Section 1 — Business in the Real World

More on Business Objectives

First Go: ...../...../.....

Factors Affecting Objectives

Size and age

_____ or _____ firms often focus on _____ satisfaction.

_____ firms may focus on the _____ and _____ acting _____.

Competition

Firms with _____ of competition often focus on customer _____ and _____.

Firms with little competition can focus on _____ and _____.

Type of business

Not-for-profit firms may focus on social and _____ objectives and _____ on profit or growth.

Ways Objectives Change

As a firm _____ and evolves, its objectives are likely to _____.

New start-up _____ focus on _____

↓

_____ business focus on _____ and maximising _____

↓

Large established business focus on having largest _____ and expansion into _____

↓

May become _____ focus on increasing _____ value

Changes in Business Environment

Businesses react to external changes by _____:

① Changes in technology
- New technology is more _____.
- Firms spend more money on _____ and training than _____.

② New legislation
- New _____ affect a firm's _____.
- Firms _____ to meet new rules, e.g. paying staff _____.

③ _____ changes
- In a recession, growth objectives are _____.
- Firm concentrates on _____.

④ Environmental expectations
- Many _____ are _____ about environmental impact.
- Firms _____ their environmental _____ to _____.

Section 1 — Business in the Real World

Second Go: ..... / ..... / .....

More on Business Objectives

Factors Affecting Objectives

Size and age

Small or new firms often

Bigger firms may

Competition

Firms with lots of

Firms with little

Type of business

Not-for-profit firms may

Ways Objectives Change

As a firm   ,
its objectives are likely to change.

New start-up
focus on

.... business
focus on

Large established business
focus on

May become
....
focus on

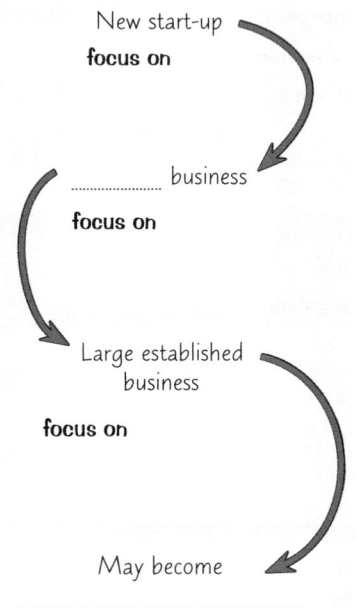

Changes in Business Environment

Businesses react to
by   :

1 Changes in technology
-
-

2 New legislation
-
- Firms adapt to
  e.g.

3
- In a recession
-

4 Environmental expectations
- Many customers are
- Firms change their

Section 1 — Business in the Real World

Stakeholders

First Go: ..... / ..... / .....

Influence of Stakeholders

STAKEHOLDER — anyone who's _____ by a business.

Businesses are also _____ by stakeholders, as their _____ must be considered when _____.

Different stakeholders can have _____, so businesses need to decide _____ in each situation.

Six Examples of Stakeholders

Shareholders get paid _____ when the firm makes _____.

Stakeholders	Like objectives based on...	Reason
① Owners / shareholders	_____ and growth	They get more _____.
② Employees	_____ and growth	Better job security and _____.
		Better _____ and _____ working conditions.
③ Suppliers	_____ and growth	They get more _____.
④ Local _____	_____ and growth	May provide _____ and mean people have more _____ to spend in _____. Local activities may be _____.
	Ethics and the _____	Local _____ isn't harmed, e.g. by _____ or _____.
⑤ Government	_____, growth and _____ creation	More money from _____.
⑥ _____	Customer satisfaction	High _____ products and low _____.

Section 1 — Business in the Real World

Second Go:
..... / ..... / .....

Stakeholders

Influence of Stakeholders

STAKEHOLDER —

Businesses are also affected by

Different stakeholders can have

Six Examples of Stakeholders

> Shareholders get paid ....

Stakeholders	Like objectives based on...	Reason
1 Owners / shareholders		
2 Employees		
	Ethics	
3		They get more custom.
4 Local community	Profitability and growth	May provide
		Local activities
		Local environment
5 Government	Profitability, growth and	
6 Customers		

Section 1 — Business in the Real World

Resources

First Go: ...../...../.....

Four Factors of Production

1 **LAND** — actual '............' and all Earth's ....

- .... resources
  E.g. oil, coal

- .... resources
  E.g. tidal power, wood

- .... materials
  E.g. gold

- Water

- ....

Nearly all resources classed as land are ....

Capital has to be made — it isn't a natural resource.

2 **CAPITAL** — equipment, ... and schools needed to .... goods or services.

3 **LABOUR** — .... done by people during the ....

Different levels of ...., experience and .... make some people more ....

4 .... — .... creating products from the other factors of production.

Providing these factors can be rewarded with ..../ rent, interest or ....

Opportunity Costs

OPPORTUNITY COST — the .... of the next best alternative that's been ....

- Most factors of production are ....

  - .... or .... spent doing one thing means missing out on doing other things.

    - Opportunity cost puts a .... on a .... in terms of what is given up.

      - Businesses can .... opportunity costs to decide the .... to use ....

Section 1 — Business in the Real World

Second Go:
..... / ..... / .....

Resources

Four Factors of Production

1) LAND —

- ....
  E.g. oil, coal
- ....
  E.g. tidal power, wood
- ....
  E.g. gold
- ....
- ....

2) CAPITAL —

Capital has to be made — it isn't a natural resource.

Nearly all ....

3) LABOUR —

Different levels of

.... can be rewarded with ...., ..., ... or ....

4) ....
— entrepreneurs creating

Opportunity Costs

OPPORTUNITY COST —

- Most factors of production
  - .... or .... spent
  - .... puts
  - Businesses can

Mixed Practice Quizzes

Have a guess what's coming next... That's right, four more quizzes that cover p.13-20. Mark your tests and set some objectives to meet your revision aims.

Quiz 1   Date: ...... / ...... / ......

1) Outline how new legislation can affect a firm's objectives.
2) True or false? Small or new firms often focus on customer satisfaction.
3) What is a stakeholder?
4) Are most factors of production limited or unlimited?
5) List four aims a business can have.
6) Suggest two objectives that firms with lots of competition may focus on.
7) What is meant by 'opportunity cost'?
8) What business aim relates to having enough money to stay open?
9) List six examples of stakeholders.
10) List five resources that are classed as 'land' factors of production.

Total:

Quiz 2   Date: ...... / ...... / ......

1) Why might employees like a business to have objectives based on ethics?
2) Name three areas of a business that may be targeted for growth.
3) What is meant by 'capital' as a factor of production?
4) True or false? Only small or new firms aim to maximise profit.
5) List three stakeholders that like objectives based on profitability and growth.
6) Outline how economic changes may affect a firm's objectives.
7) What three things would the government like firms to base objectives on?
8) List three factors that can affect a business's objectives.
9) Explain why a business should compare opportunity costs.
10) How do the objectives of a new start-up change as they evolve into a stable business?

Total:

Mixed Practice Quizzes

Quiz 3 Date: …… / …… / ……

1) How may firms spend money in reaction to changes in technology?
2) List the four factors of production.
3) What objectives may firms with little competition focus on?
4) Give two ways a firm can aim to increase market share.
5) What stakeholder likes objectives that lead to more money from taxes?
6) Suggest how a firm's objectives are affected by environmental expectations.
7) What kind of firm would focus on increasing shareholder value?
8) What is meant by 'labour'?
9) True or false? An objective is a measurable step that a business uses to work towards an aim.
10) How could the local community benefit when a firm focuses on growth?

Total:

Quiz 4 Date: …… / …… / ……

1) True or false? In terms of growth, a firm can only aim domestically.
2) Why do suppliers like objectives based on profitability and growth?
3) What is meant by a business 'aim'?
4) List three things that affect the productivity of labour.
5) What would a business's shareholders like its objectives to be based on?
6) How can a business aim of customer satisfaction be measured?
7) Which factor of production uses the other three factors to create products?
8) What kind of objectives are not-for-profit firms likely to focus on?
9) Why do shareholders get more money if a firm is very profitable?
10) List four external changes that cause firms to change their objectives.

Total:

Revenue, Costs and Profit

First Go: ...../...../.....

Revenue

REVENUE — .... businesses make by ....

revenue = ... × ....

EXAMPLE

The stationery company Jot It Down sells 10 000 notebooks for £5 each. What is their sales revenue?

revenue = ... × £5 = £............

Costs

FIXED COSTS — costs that don't .... with output, e.g. .... , ... , advertising.

.... costs are paid even if the business produces ....

Fixed costs are only fixed in the .... term — they .... as the business grows.

VARIABLE COSTS — costs that increase as .... increases, e.g. factory labour, raw .... , running ....

total cost = total .... cost + total .... cost

The total cost is the sum of the .... costs and .... costs.

Average Unit Cost

Average unit costs usually .... as a firm ....

- Average unit cost is how much each .... costs to ....

  average unit cost = ... cost ÷ ....

- To make a profit, the firm must charge a .... price than the ....

EXAMPLE

The total cost for Jot It Down to produce 3000 calculators is £9000. What is the average unit cost?

average unit cost = £............ ÷ 3000 = £............

Profit and Loss

PROFIT — the .... between .... and costs over a period of time.

profit = ... − ....

If costs are higher than revenue, the business makes .... — the amount of profit is ....

EXAMPLE

In May, Jot It Down has a revenue of £10 000, and has total costs of £4000. How much profit does Jot It Down make in May?

profit = £10 000 − £............ = £............

Section 1 — Business in the Real World

Revenue, Costs and Profit

Second Go: ..... / ..... / .....

Revenue

REVENUE —

revenue =

EXAMPLE

The stationery company Jot It Down sells 10 000 notebooks for £5 each. What is their sales revenue?

revenue =   =

Costs

> Fixed costs are ....

FIXED COSTS —

Fixed costs are only

VARIABLE COSTS — costs that

The total cost is

total cost = ...
....

Average Unit Cost

> Average unit costs usually ....

- Average unit cost is

    average unit cost =
    ....

EXAMPLE

The total cost for Jot It Down to produce 3000 calculators is £9000. What is the average unit cost?

average unit cost = ... = ...

- To make a profit,

Profit and Loss

PROFIT —

profit =

If costs are higher

EXAMPLE

In May, Jot It Down has a revenue of £10 000, and has total costs of £4000. How much profit does Jot It Down make in May?

profit =
=

Section 1 — Business in the Real World

The Business Plan

First Go: ...../...../......

Four Reasons for Business Plans

BUSINESS PLAN — an outline of .... a business will do and .... it will do it.

> They can be used to plan .... businesses or make changes to .... businesses.

1 Forces .... to think carefully about the business's ...., organisation and necessary ....
↳ Owner can work out how much .... is needed.

2 Convinces .... that it's a good ....

3 Identifies if it's a .... early on — before time and money are ....

4 Helps to decide .... needed to achieve the business's ....

Sections of Business Plans

.... of owner and any key personnel, e.g. their CVs.

Mission statement — describes the .... of the business, e.g. to become market .... in their sector.

Objectives are .... more .... than aims, e.g. a sales ....

Finance — money needed to .... for things like ...., profit, ...

[BUSINESS PLAN: Geraldine's Ices]

Product Description — including .... strategy and how the .... will be achieved.

.... details — how the product is made or the service is provided, including .... needed and ....

Staffing requirements — .... of staff, their job descriptions, expected ....

.... the business and ....

Three Drawbacks of Business Plans

1 Plans take .... and .... to write. ⟹ The benefit may not .... the cost.

2 The plan may be too .... ⟹ If .... are lower than predicted, the business may struggle to ....

3 Firms may .... to the plan. ⟹ Not .... the plan for .... can cause problems.

Section 1 — Business in the Real World

The Business Plan

Second Go: ...../...../.....

Four Reasons for Business Plans

BUSINESS PLAN —

They can be used to ....

1) Forces owner to

↘ Owner can

2) Convinces

3) Identifies if

4) Helps to decide

Sections of Business Plans

Mission statement —

e.g.

Product Description —

Production details —

Finance —

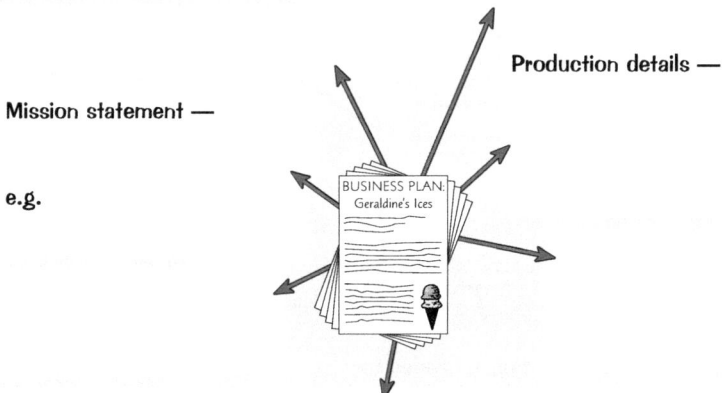

Three Drawbacks of Business Plans

1) Plans take

2) The plan may → If sales are

3) Firms may → Not .... the plan

The benefit

Section 1 — Business in the Real World

Location

First Go: ..... / ..... / .....

Raw Materials

Locating .... to raw materials means lower ....

E.g. a jam manufacturer may locate .... a farm or orchard.

Labour Supply

- Areas with high unemployment have .... and good ....
- Towns and cities might have colleges that can provide ....

Market Location

Locating near customers has benefits:

1 Cheaper to .... finished product if customers are ....

2 Some .... locate where people can .... get to them. E.g. pharmacies are often on the high street.

3 Global firms may set up their .... in countries with a ....

- Reduces .... costs.
- No import ....

Businesses that trade over the .... can be more .... about their location.

Cost

- .... varies between countries.

- .... of renting or buying premises .... between different areas.

- Governments might give .... or .... to firms located in areas of high ....

Competition

Being .... competitors has advantages and disadvantages.

➕ Advantages

- Easy to find ....
- Existing local ....
- Customers know ....

➖ Disadvantage

Loss of .... to competitors

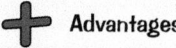

Section 1 — Business in the Real World

Second Go:
..... /..... /.....

Location

Raw Materials

Locating near

E.g. a jam manufacturer may locate

Market Location

Locating near customers has benefits:

① Cheaper to transport

② Some services locate

E.g. pharmacies are often on the

③ Global firms may

- Reduces
- No

Competition

Being near competitors has advantages and disadvantages.

 Advantages

- Easy to
- Existing
-

Labour Supply

- Areas with high unemployment

- Towns and cities might have

Businesses that trade ....
....
....
....

Cost

-

- Price of

- Governments might give

━━ Disadvantage

Section 1 — Business in the Real World

Mixed Practice Quizzes

Some more quizzes here, to test you on p.23-28. The total box is conveniently located after each quiz — so put your score there once you've marked them.

Quiz 1   Date: ...... / ...... / ......

1) True or false? The government may give grants to firms located in areas of high unemployment.
2) If a business is making a loss, which is higher — its costs or its revenue?
3) Outline what the staffing requirements section of a business plan contains.
4) Outline one way labour supply affects where a business locates.
5) Suggest when a business can be more flexible about their location.
6)* The total cost for a firm to produce 50 smartphones is £10 000. What is the average unit cost?
7) What can happen if a business plan is too optimistic?
8) How can you calculate a firm's profit from its revenue and costs?
9) Give four reasons why a firm would make a business plan.
10) How do you calculate the total cost for a firm?

Total:

Quiz 2   Date: ...... / ...... / ......

1) What is the mission statement on a business plan?
2) Outline two ways that cost influences where a business locates.
3) True or false? A business plan is only useful for planning new businesses.
4) Give two benefits to a firm locating near its customers.
5) What type of costs must a firm pay even if it doesn't produce anything?
6) What is the formula to calculate average unit cost?
7)* One year, an ice cream shop has total costs of £32 000 and has a revenue of £44 000. What is the shop's profit?
8) Give one disadvantage to a firm locating near to its competitors.
9) Define 'profit'.
10) What should be included in the finance section of a business plan?

Total:

Section 1 — Business in the Real World

Mixed Practice Quizzes

Quiz 3   Date: ...... / ...... / ......

1) List three advantages to a firm being located near to its competitors.
2) True or false? A firm's fixed costs never change, even when the firm grows.
3) What does the production details section on a business plan describe?
4) Outline one way a business can reduce transport costs when deciding on a location.
5) What usually happens to average unit costs as a firm grows?
6) Give an example of a service that is often located near to its customers.
7) Explain why firms should not stick too tightly to a business plan.
8) What section of a business plan would contain the CVs of owners and any key personnel?
9)* A firm sells 500 TVs for £200 each. What is the sales revenue?
10) True or false? A firm must charge a lower price than the average unit cost to make a profit.

Total:

Quiz 4   Date: ...... / ...... / ......

1) Define 'revenue'.
2) What is a business plan?
3)* One month, a bakery has total fixed costs of £6000 and total variable costs of £7500. Calculate the bakery's total costs for the month.
4) Why may a firm locate to areas of high unemployment?
5) List six sections of a business plan.
6) True or false? A loss is the same as a negative profit.
7) Give two benefits to a global firm setting up their production in countries with a large market.
8) What are variable costs?
9) Why may a business locate near to raw materials?
10) Give three drawbacks of business plans.

Total:

Expanding Businesses

First Go: ..... / ..... / .....

Economies of Scale

Bigger firms make .... products and have more .... This can lead to economies of scale.

ECONOMY OF SCALE — when there is a .... in .... due to producing on a .... scale.

Lower average .... → More .... per sale

↳ Firm can afford to ....

↳ Increased ....

↳ Increased ....

Increase in .... due to economies of scale can fund further ....

Diseconomies of Scale

DISECONOMY OF SCALE — an .... in average .... due to a business being ....

Reasons for diseconomies of scale:

1 Management

Bigger businesses are .... and .... to manage.

3 Employees

Larger firms have more .... , so harder to ....

- Takes .... for .... to reach workforce.
- Employees at .... of organisational structure can feel ....
- Workers can be .... , lowering ....

Purchasing Economies of Scale

Firm buys supplies in ....

↳ Cheaper ....

↳ Lower ....

Technical Economies of Scale

- Bigger firms can afford to buy and operate more .... machinery.

  ↳ Machinery is more .... to run.

  ↳ Lower ....

- Bigger firms often have larger ....

  ↳ Cheaper per .... than smaller ....

E.g. a factory that is 10 times bigger is .... than 10 times as expensive.

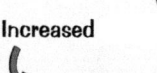

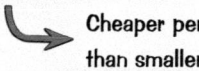

2 ....

Production processes are usually .... and difficult to .... for larger firms.

Second Go: ..... /..... /.....

Expanding Businesses

Economies of Scale

Bigger firms

This can lead to economies of scale.

ECONOMY OF SCALE — when there is a

Lower → More

Increase in

Purchasing Economies of Scale

Firm buys

Technical Economies of Scale

- Bigger firms can afford to

- Bigger firms often have

E.g. a factory that is 10 times bigger is

② Production

Diseconomies of Scale

DISECONOMY OF SCALE —

Reasons for diseconomies of scale:
① Management
Bigger businesses are

③ Employees
Larger firms have more
-
-
-

Section 1 — Business in the Real World

Internal Expansion

First Go: ...../...../.....

Advantages and Disadvantages of Internal Expansion

INTERNAL EXPANSION — when a business .... by expanding its own ....

➕ **Advantages**
- fairly ....
- low ....
- slower .... makes it .... easier to maintain and train staff

Internal expansion generally involves a firm doing .... of what it's already ....

➖ **Disadvantage**
- .... takes a .... to achieve growth

Internal expansion can also be called .... growth.

Methods of Internal Expansion

	➕ Advantages	➖ Disadvantages
Selling	• customers don't need to be .... a shop .... — .... market • no .... and .... staff needed than a physical store	• .... issues can frustrate customers • technology needs regular ....
Opening new stores	• low .... — likely a .... if similar to existing stores	• .... e.g. rent, staff pay
.... — paying another firm to carry out tasks that could be done	Tasks might be done... • .... • cheaper .... • .... to a better	• less .... • outsourcing firm has other .... and priorities • standards of outsourcing firm will affect ....

Franchising

FRANCHISING — one firm lets other firms .... its products (or use its ....) in return for a fee or percentage of ....
- The product manufacturer is a ....
- A firm selling the franchisor's products is a ....

➕
- increased .... for franchisor
- more .... share and brand awareness
- franchisee responsible for the .... and .... of running a new outlet

➖ brand can get a bad .... if the franchisee has poor ....

Section 1 — Business in the Real World

Internal Expansion

Second Go: ..../..../....

Advantages and Disadvantages of Internal Expansion

INTERNAL EXPANSION —   Disadvantage

Advantages
-
-
- slower pace of growth makes it

> Internal expansion generally involves ....

> Internal expansion can ....

Methods of Internal Expansion

	Advantages	Disadvantages
	• customers don't need •	• • technology needs
Opening new stores	• .... —	• extra
.... — paying another firm to	Tasks might be done... • • •	• • outsourcing firm has • standards of

Franchising

FRANCHISING —

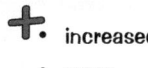
- increased
- more
-

- The product manufacturer is
- A firm selling

— brand can get a

External Expansion

First Go: ..... /..... /.....

Mergers and Takeovers

Two ways of achieving external expansion:

1) MERGER — _____ firms _____ to form a new, _____ firm.

2) _____ — an existing firm _____ by buying _____ the shares in another firm.

External expansion means the business _____ much more _____ than _____ with internal expansion.

Four Ways Mergers or Takeovers Happen

1) Firm joins with a _____.

Firm controls the _____, cost and _____ of its raw materials.

2) Firm takes over one of its _____.

E.g. a manufacturer takes over a chain of retail outlets.

Firm has greater _____ to the _____.

3) A firm joins with one of its competitors.

Firm has more _____ and gets a bigger _____.

So it's a stronger _____.

4) Two unrelated firms join.

Firm diversifies into _____, reducing risk from relying on few _____.

Problems with Mergers and Takeovers

- Can create _____ — some takeovers are _____ and _____.

- Hard to make two different businesses _____. → _____ style or culture might differ. This can lead to _____ employees.

- Can lead to _____. → This might involve _____, leading to tension and _____ among workers.

Most takeovers and mergers are _____.

Section 1 — Business in the Real World

External Expansion

Mergers and Takeovers

Two ways of achieving external expansion:

1 MERGER — two firms

2 TAKEOVER — an existing firm

External expansion means

3 A firm joins with one of its competitors.

Four Ways Mergers or Takeovers Happen

1 Firm joins with a supplier.

Firm controls

2 Firm takes over one of its ....

E.g. a manufacturer takes over a chain of retail outlets.

Firm has

4 ....

Firm diversifies into

Problems with Mergers and Takeovers

- Can create .... — some

- Hard to

-

....
....
....

Management style or

This might involve ...., leading to

Mixed Practice Quizzes

Find out if your business knowledge has expanded with these quizzes that test p.31-36. Mark each quiz yourself and work out your total score.

Quiz 1 — Date: ...... / ...... / ......

1) Give one disadvantage of internal expansion.
2) Give two different ways in which firms can achieve external expansion.
3) True or false? Bigger businesses are harder and more expensive to manage.
4) Why can mergers and takeovers lead to redundancies?
5) What is meant by 'franchising'?
6) What term describes a reduction of average unit costs due to producing on a large scale?
7) Give two disadvantages to a firm expanding to sell online.
8) What is outsourcing?
9) List four ways that a merger or takeover can happen.
10) Give two possible reasons for economies of scale in large firms.

Total:

Quiz 2 — Date: ...... / ...... / ......

1) Give three advantages of franchising.
2) What is meant by 'diseconomy of scale'?
3) What is a takeover?
4) How can a firm expand externally to diversify into new markets?
5) Give three methods of internal expansion.
6) True or false? A firm having larger premises can lead to economies of scale.
7) What extra costs are involved for a firm when opening new stores?
8) In franchising, what is the name of the product manufacturer?
9) Give one advantage of external expansion.
10) Explain why it is hard to make two different businesses work as one after external expansion.

Total:

Section 1 — Business in the Real World

Mixed Practice Quizzes

Quiz 3 Date: ...... / ...... / ......

1) What is meant by 'economy of scale'?
2) True or false? Most takeovers and mergers are unsuccessful.
3) Give three advantages of internal expansion.
4) Give one advantage of a firm taking over one of its customers.
5) List three disadvantages of outsourcing.
6) What is another name for internal expansion?
7) Give two ways in which having more employees can lead to diseconomies of scale.
8) True or false? Only small or new firms can achieve economies of scale.
9) Outline the benefits of a firm growing by joining with one of its suppliers.
10) How can buying more advanced machinery lead to a lower average unit cost for a firm?

Total:

Quiz 4 Date: ...... / ...... / ......

1) What is internal expansion?
2) Explain two possible reasons for diseconomies of scale in large firms.
3) Give one advantage of a firm joining with one of its competitors.
4) Outline one way technical economies of scale can happen for a big firm.
5) Give one disadvantage of franchising.
6) What is a merger?
7) Explain how buying in bulk affects the average unit cost.
8) List three advantages to a firm expanding to sell online.
9) True or false? A lower average unit cost means firms can afford to lower prices, which can lead to an increase in sales.
10) Give three problems with mergers and takeovers.

Total:

Section 1 — Business in the Real World

Section 2 — Influences on Business

Businesses and the Law

First Go: ...../...../......

Pay

There's a _____ that firms need to pay their workers:
- National _____ Wage — for workers _____, of school leaving age.
- National _____ Wage — for workers aged _____.

+ Potentially better _____ staff and higher _____.

− Can _____ business costs, meaning: _____ prices → _____ sales → _____ income

Discrimination

Equality Act (2010) — employers can't _____ against anyone because of:
- race
- sexual orientation
- religion
- _____
- gender

This affects _____ and pay — staff must be paid _____ for doing the same job, or work of _____.

Firms write _____ and train staff about _____.

Consumer Law

Consumer Rights Act 2015 — covers how products can be _____.

Three criteria a product must meet:

1. Be _____ for _____ — it has to do the job it was _____ for.

2. Match its _____ — it must match how the business describes it (_____ description), e.g. _____, quantity, materials.
   It's illegal to _____ it's endorsed by a person or organisation.

3. Be of satisfactory _____ — it should be well made and shouldn't cause problems for the buyer.

Health and Safety

Health and Safety at Work Act (1974) — firms must:
- carry out _____ to identify workplace _____.
- take reasonable steps to _____.
- provide staff with health and safety _____ and suitable _____.

+ Reduces staff _____, so a more _____ workforce.

− _____ for businesses (e.g. paying for training courses).

Impacts of Breaking Laws

Consumer law:
- Customers can ask for a _____, repair or _____.
- Customers could take the business to _____, which can be very _____.
- The business could get a _____ reputation, which could reduce _____.

Employment law:
- _____ costs
- _____
- Bad _____
- _____ of the firm

Section 2 — Influences on Business

Businesses and the Law

Second Go:
..... / ..... / .....

Pay

There's a _____ that firms need to pay their workers:
- National Minimum Wage — _____
- National Living Wage — _____

+ Potentially better _____

— Can _____ business costs, meaning:
→ _____
→ _____

Discrimination

_____ employers can't discriminate against anyone because of:
-
-
-
-
-
-

This affects recruitment and pay — _____

Health and Safety

Health and Safety at Work Act (1974) — firms must:
- carry out _____
- take _____
- provide staff with _____

Firms write _____

+

—

Consumer Law

_____ covers how products can be sold. Three criteria a product must meet:

1. _____

2. Match its description — _____

   It's illegal to _____

3. Be of satisfactory _____

Impacts of Breaking Laws

Consumer law:
- Customers can ask for _____
- Customers could take _____
- The business could get a _____

Employment law:
-
-
-
-

Section 2 — Influences on Business

Technology and Business

First Go: ..... / ..... / .....

Impact of Changing Technology

ICT includes things such as   , phone networks and the   .

+
- Computers can do jobs more   . → Reduced long-term —
- People can   more easily.   are needed to do tasks.

−
- New equipment is   to buy.
- Staff need to be   or   to use new technology.

E-Commerce

E-COMMERCE — buying and   products using the   .

Firms need to   to the growing need to use   by e.g.:

+ Good for   as they can reach   .

- building
- employing   ,
- developing ways to   to online customers.

Six Methods of Digital Communication

1) Websites
Useful for a wide range of   . E.g. can provide   for customers and publish   for shareholders.

2) Apps
Used to   and   with customers, e.g. about promotions.

3) Social media
Good way to   with a   of people. Used for   and promotion, e.g. to advertise products or   .

4) Email
             and   way to communicate either with   or a   .

5) Video calls
Convenient way to have   with stakeholders based in different   , e.g.   on different sites.

6) Live chats
often used for   and communication between   .

Section 2 — Influences on Business

Technology and Business

Second Go: ...../...../.....

Impact of Changing Technology

ICT includes things such as

+
- Computers
- People can

→ Reduced long-term

−
- New equipment
- Staff need to be

E-Commerce

E-COMMERCE —

+ Good for firms

Firms need to adapt to the growing need to use e-commerce by e.g.:

-
-
-

Six Methods of Digital Communication

1) Websites

Useful for

E.g.

2) Apps

Used to

e.g.

3) Social media

Good way to

Used for

4) Email

Quick and easy way to

5) Video calls

Convenient way to

e.g.

6) Live chats

Section 2 — Influences on Business

Ethical Considerations

First Go: ..... /..... /.....

Acting Ethically

ETHICS — the moral principles of _____ .

Ethical issues are important, so many businesses try to _____ .

Overseas employees

Firms can write _____ to _____ the number of hours for workers in overseas _____ / _____ .

In some countries, it's not illegal for people to work long hours for low pay.

UK employees

Firms can:
- _____ staff fairly
- keep _____ safe
- provide a _____ working environment

Buying raw materials

Firms can buy raw materials from _____ sources, so workers from _____ countries earn _____ .

Promoting products

Firms follow codes of practice to not criticise _____ .

Some products can't be _____ at all, e.g. _____ .

Product development

Firms can choose _____ materials for their products and not test on _____ .

Balancing Ethics and Profit

Businesses have their own _____ — these are ways of working that _____ think are fair and _____ .

But there's a _____ between acting ethically and making the most _____ .

Advantages of acting ethically

- can be used to _____ products
- can attract _____
- appeals to _____ /investors
- staff more _____ and productive

Disadvantages of acting ethically

- expensive — firms may have to _____ for staff and _____
- may be hard to find ethical _____
- lower _____ per product sold

Section 2 — Influences on Business

Second Go: ..... / ..... / .....

Ethical Considerations

Acting Ethically

ETHICS —

Ethical issues are important, so

Overseas employees	UK employees
Firms can write	Firms can:
	•
	•
	•

Buying raw materials	Promoting products	Product development
Firms can	Firms follow	Firms can choose
so workers from	Some products	

Balancing Ethics and Profit

Businesses have their own ethical policies —

But there's a trade-off

Advantages of acting ethically	Disadvantages of acting ethically
• can be used	• expensive —
•	
• appeals to	•
• staff	• Lower

Section 2 — Influences on Business

Environmental Influences

First Go: ..... / ..... / .....

Five Ways to Reduce Environmental Impacts

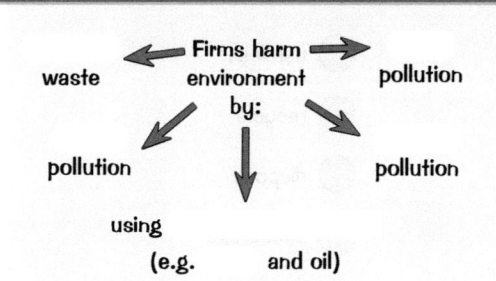

waste ← Firms harm → pollution
environment by:
↙ ↓ ↘
pollution pollution
using
(e.g. _____ and oil)

1. use less _____
2. _____ unwanted goods
3. dispose of _____ responsibly
4. encourage _____ schemes or _____ to work
5. buy quieter _____ or use _____

Global Impact of Business

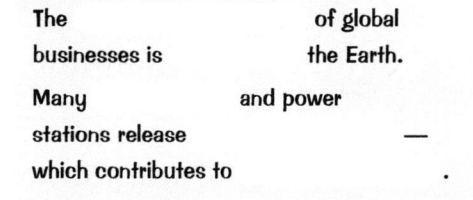

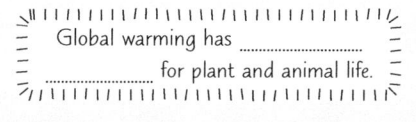

The _____ of global businesses is _____ the Earth.

Many _____ and power stations release _____ which contributes to _____.

Global warming has _____ _____ for plant and animal life.

More carbon dioxide in _____ → Climate becomes _____ → _____ melt — sea levels rise, more flooding

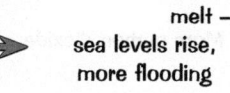

Sustainable Business

Many firms want to be more _____ — working in a way _____ to not damage the Earth for _____, e.g.:

using _____ energy resources

using less-polluting _____

using more _____ electrical goods

Advantages
- appeals to _____ interested in being _____
- can give competitive _____

Disadvantage

more sustainable _____ and new _____ can be _____ — this may lead to lower _____

Section 2 — Influences on Business

Environmental Influences

Second Go:
..... / ..... / .....

Five Ways to Reduce Environmental Impacts

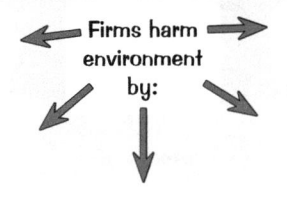

← Firms harm →
environment
by:
↙ ↓ ↘

1. use less
2. recycle
3. dispose
4. encourage
5. buy quieter

Global Impact of Business

The combined impact

Many industries

Global warming ....
....
....

Ice caps

More carbon dioxide → Climate becomes →

Sustainable Business

Many firms want to be more sustainable —

E.g.

Advantages
- appeals to

- can give

Disadvantage
more sustainable processes

Section 2 — Influences on Business

Mixed Practice Quizzes

Right, four more quizzes to test what you know about p.39-46. If you prefer the trade description: 40 great questions over two pages, typeset in black, 10 pt...

Quiz 1   Date: ...... / ...... / ......

1) What does 'satisfactory quality' mean in terms of consumer law?
2) What does a firm have in order to ensure it works in ways that stakeholders think are fair?
3) What is e-commerce?
4) Give five ways businesses may harm the environment.
5) Explain how minimum wage laws could lead to reduced sales for a business.
6) Give two ways that a business could use social media to communicate.
7) True or false? A firm can work in a more sustainable way by using renewable energy resources.
8) How can a business act ethically when developing products?
9) How does the Equality Act 2010 affect pay?
10) Give one reason why a website can be useful for a firm's stakeholders.

Total:

Quiz 2   Date: ...... / ...... / ......

1) What is meant by 'ethics'?
2) Give one negative effect of health and safety laws on businesses.
3) What changes to machinery could a firm make to be more sustainable?
4) Give two ways that a firm could adapt to the need to use e-commerce.
5) True or false? It's legal for firms to falsely claim that their product has been endorsed by someone when they are promoting it.
6) Give two non-renewables used by firms.
7) Give three disadvantages to a firm of acting ethically.
8) How could new technology reduce costs for a business in the long term?
9) Give three potential impacts on a business of breaking employment laws.
10) Explain one disadvantage to a firm of working in a more sustainable way.

Total:

Section 2 — Influences on Business

Mixed Practice Quizzes

Quiz 3 Date: ...... / ...... / ......

1) What does it mean for a firm to be 'sustainable'?
2) What three criteria must products meet under the Consumer Rights Act 2015?
3) Give one ethical consideration for a firm when promoting a product.
4) Outline why video calls are a useful method of communication for firms.
5) Give two potential impacts on a firm of breaking consumer law.
6) Give one advantage to a business of using e-commerce.
7) What do many industries release into the environment that contributes to global warming?
8) Give one potential benefit of minimum wage laws to businesses.
9) State four methods of digital communication used by businesses.
10) Give four advantages to a firm of acting ethically.

Total:

Quiz 4 Date: ...... / ...... / ......

1) List six things that the Equality Act (2010) says employers can't discriminate against.
2) True or false? Firms might need to balance acting ethically and making a profit.
3) Give one disadvantage of changing technology for a business.
4) Give five ways a firm can reduce its impact on the environment.
5) Outline how a firm can act ethically in relation to its employees.
6) Give one benefit of buying raw materials from Fairtrade sources.
7) Give two ways that live chats could be useful to a business.
8) What are the two minimum levels of pay in the UK?
9) Give two advantages to a firm of working in a more sustainable way.
10) Give three actions that firms take to comply with health and safety laws.

Total:

Businesses and the Economic Climate

First Go: ...../...../.....

Unemployment

.... of people unemployed. → People have .... to spend. → Demand for product sales .... → Firms respond, e.g. by reducing .... or making staff ....

But there are potential benefits:

1. Less money spent on .... — people may be prepared to .... for .... money.
2. Easier to .... — there are lots of people available to work.
3. Government .... to firms who provide jobs in areas of high ....

Consumer Income

The amount consumers .... increases over ....

If prices rise at a .... rate than income... → Greater proportion of people's .... spent on .... items, e.g. food.

Less money available for .... , e.g. holidays, so demand for these ....

Businesses selling .... see fall in .... and ....

The opposite is true when income rises at a .... rate than prices rise.

Interest Rate Changes

INTEREST RATE — a .... that shows the cost of .... money or the .... given for saving money.

Amount needing to be .... on existing .... money may also ....

If interest rate is cut... → Cheaper to .... money. Less money made on ....

.... interest rates Increased spending

.... interest rates Decreased spending

Consumers .... more and save .... They have more money to ....

↓

.... for products goes up.

↓

Sales and profits ....

Businesses .... more. They have more money to .... in the business.

↓

Increased investment leads to ....

The opposite is true when interest rates .... — .... for products goes .... , and businesses have .... money. This may lead to .... growth and ....

Section 2 — Influences on Business

50

Second Go:
..... /..... /.....

Businesses and the Economic Climate

Unemployment

Lots of people → People have less → Demand → Firms respond, e.g.

But there are potential benefits:

1. Less money spent on
2. Easier to
3. Government

Consumer Income

The amount consumers

If prices rise → Greater proportion

Less money

Businesses selling

Interest Rate Changes

INTEREST RATE —

The opposite is true when

Amount needing to be ....

If interest rate is cut...

Cheaper
Less

.... interest rates
Increased ....

.... interest rates
Decreased ....

Consumers borrow

Businesses borrow

Demand

Increased

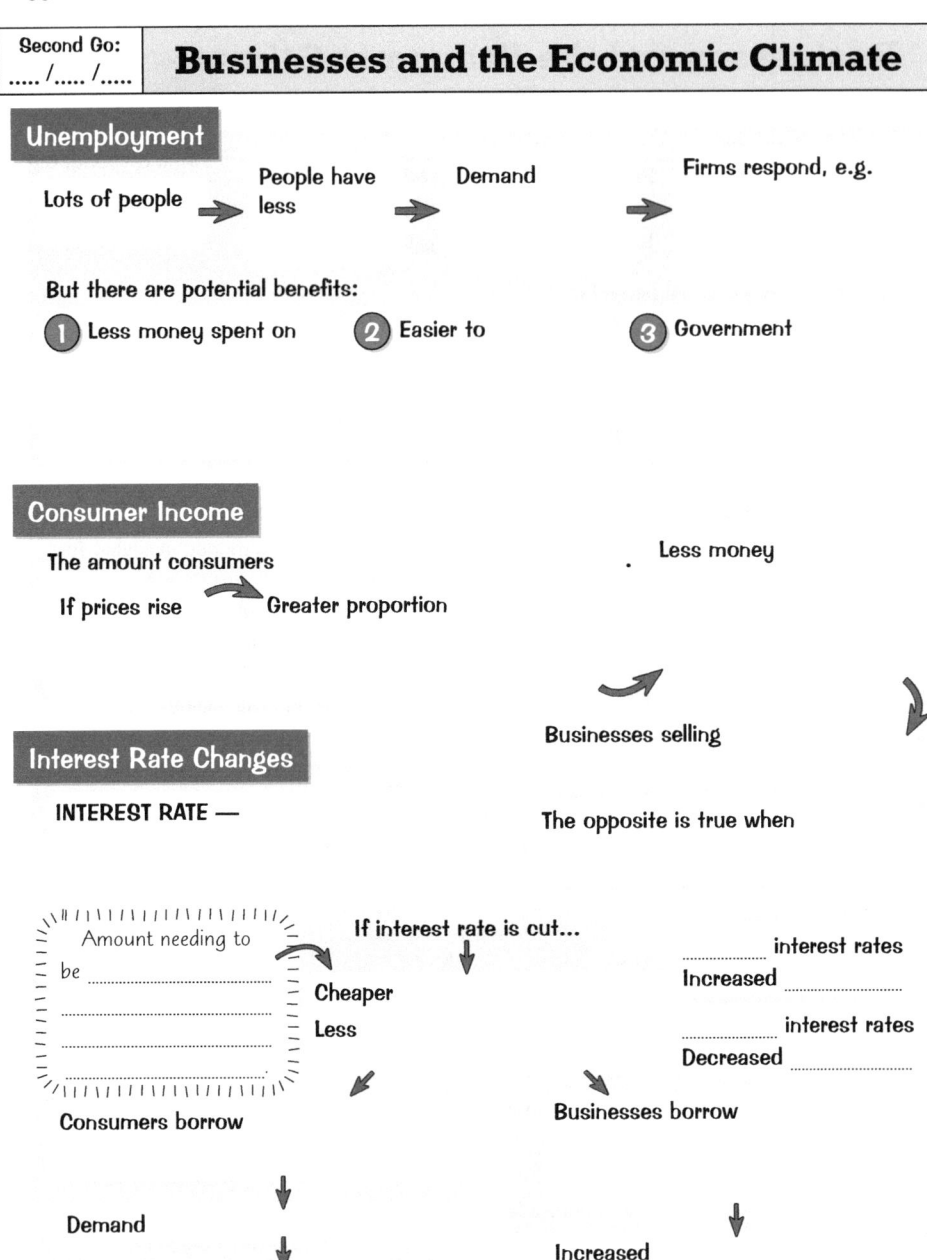

The opposite is true when interest rates increase —

Section 2 — Influences on Business

Competition

First Go: ...../...../.....

Markets

The word market can mean:

1. a place where .... are traded.

2. trade in a particular ....

3. the .... for a product.

Competitive Markets

COMPETITOR — a .... that sells the same .... in the same .... as another business.

Competitive markets have .... — a large number of producers selling to a large number of ....

Effects on a business in a competitive market:

- Can't .... — charging too much will mean consumers go elsewhere.
  ↳ So firms have to make ....

- Customers need .... — firms have to .... customers that their product is .... than their rivals'.
  ↳ So firms spend more on, e.g. .... and developing ....

- Firms look to fill any ....
  ↳ So firms spend lots on .... new products.

Lots of .... means firms often make the .... product.

Competition only over product's .... → Prices and .... driven .... → .... to develop new, better products.

Three Markets with Minimal Competition

1. When a firm .... a brand new product, there won't be any competition.
   If .... want the product, they have to ....

2. .... products will have ....
   The market won't be .... for many businesses to survive.

3. Some markets are .... to start a business in.
   There will be .... as few businesses can .... the cost.

Section 2 — Influences on Business

Second Go: ..... / ..... / .....

Competition

Markets

The word market can mean:

1.

2.

3.

Competitive Markets

COMPETITOR —

Competitive markets have

Effects on a business in a competitive market:

- Can't dictate prices —
  ↳ So firms have to make

- Customers need convincing —
  ↳ So firms spend

- Firms look to fill
  ↳ So firms spend

Lots of competition means

Competition → Prices → Less money

Three Markets with Minimal Competition

1. When a firm launches

2. Specialist products

3. Some markets

Section 2 — Influences on Business

Globalisation and Exchange Rates

First Go: ..... / ..... / .....

International Trade

GLOBALISATION — the process by which .... around the world become ....

Import = ... goods from abroad.
Export = ... goods abroad.

UK businesses compete internationally by:

- investing in the .... of new .... or processes.
- maintaining high quality ...., while keeping prices .... than competitors.

Effects of Globalisation

+ Advantages

- .... market means increased .... and .... supplies
- setting up .... near .... reduces .... costs and import ....
- labour can be .... overseas

− Disadvantages

- average UK wage is ...., so hard to .... with other countries
- potential of .... if seen to be .... workers overseas
- .... can be affected by changes in ....

Exchange Rate Basics

EXCHANGE RATE — the .... at which one currency can be .... for another.

Exchange rates .... — they are affected by the economy of the .... that uses the currency, and by the global ....

Value of the Pound

Fall in £ value ↗ good for ....

- UK products sold abroad get .... to buy abroad. → .... sales and .... for firms that export a lot.
- Foreign products sold in the UK get more .... → Costs .... for UK firms importing .... → May need to increase .... Profits may ....

Rise in £ value ↗ good for ....

- UK products sold abroad get .... to buy abroad. → .... sales and profits for firms that .... a lot.
- Foreign products sold in the UK get .... → Costs .... for UK firms .... raw materials. → Profits may ....

☹ ✓   😐 ✓   🙂 ✓   Section 2 — Influences on Business

Second Go:
..... / ..... / .....

Globalisation and Exchange Rates

International Trade

GLOBALISATION —

Import = ...
....
Export = ...
....

UK businesses compete internationally by:
- investing
- maintaining

Effects of Globalisation

✚ Advantages
- larger market
- setting up factories
- labour can

➖ Disadvantages
- average UK wage
- potential of
- profits

Exchange Rate Basics

EXCHANGE RATE —

Exchange rates fluctuate —

Value of the Pound

Fall in £ value ↗ UK products → Increased sales
↘ Foreign products → Costs increase → May need to

Rise in £ value ↗ UK products → Decreased sales
↘ Foreign products → Costs decrease → Profits may

Section 2 — Influences on Business

Risks in Business

First Go: ...../...../.....

Three Risks for Businesses

All businesses face   and   :

1 Starting a business
- Entrepreneurs need money for   and   .
- They may use their   and borrow from   and   .
-              must be made to   money   or the firm will fail.

2 Health of the economy
- Affects   levels,   rates and   rates.
- Changes can affect   for products and   in a business.

3 Actions of competitors
- Competitors may bring out   .
- Firms may   if they lose   to competitors.

Planning to Reduce Risk

- Do a proper   .

-                        in order to   or   the business.

- Have   in place for   ,
e.g. what to do if a supplier   .

Researching to Reduce Risk

Research helps businesses   for changes and put   for dealing with them.

- Carry out regular   — to check the   is right for their products.

- Research the   — to be aware of competitors,   and   changes.

- Research   changes to the   — e.g. from planned changes to the   .

Section 2 — Influences on Business

Second Go: ..... /..... /.....

Risks in Business

Three Risks for Businesses

All businesses face   and   :

1. Starting ....
   - Entrepreneurs
   - They may use
   - Profits must

2. Health ....
   - Affects
   - Changes

3. Actions ....
   - Competitors
   - Firms may

Planning to Reduce Risk

- Do

- Make

- Have plan Bs

Researching to Reduce Risk

Research helps businesses

- Carry out regular .... research —

- Research the .... —

- Research predicted changes to the .... —

Section 2 — Influences on Business

Mixed Practice Quizzes

That's Section 2 sorted, so try these quizzes covering p.49-56. Have a go at each quiz, ~~market~~ mark it yourself and move on when your interest is high enough.

Quiz 1 — Date: ...... / ...... / ......

1) What is an 'interest rate'?
2) True or false? Making a business plan helps to reduce risk.
3) Give one factor that causes fluctuation in exchange rates.
4) Give three meanings of the term 'market'.
5) Why might firms find it easier to recruit when unemployment is high?
6) Give one potential effect of the value of the pound increasing.
7) True or false? A business in a competitive market can easily dictate prices.
8) Give one risk an entrepreneur may face when starting a business.
9) Why do consumers have more money to spend when interest rates are low?
10) Give two advantages of globalisation for businesses.

Total:

Quiz 2 — Date: ...... / ...... / ......

1) What is meant by 'exchange rate'?
2) List three things that a business may research to reduce risk.
3) Give one effect of a competitive market on a business.
4) Explain how a rise in the value of the pound affects importers.
5) Why might firms spend less on wages when unemployment is high?
6) Give an example of a scenario when a business may need to use a 'plan B'.
7) True or false? Higher interest rates are likely to lead to slower business growth.
8) Give two examples of markets that have low competition.
9) Explain how the actions of competitors are a risk for a business.
10) What could happen to the demand for luxury goods if prices rise at a faster rate than consumer income?

Total:

Section 2 — Influences on Business

Mixed Practice Quizzes

Quiz 3 Date: ...... / ...... / ......

1) What is a competitor?
2) Give two actions that UK businesses take to compete internationally.
3) Explain how a cut in interest rates could lead to better sales for a firm.
4) What is the name for the process by which businesses and countries around the world become more connected?
5) Explain why research can reduce the risks of a running a business.
6) Outline why a business in a competitive market should make production efficient.
7) Give one effect of consumer income rising at a faster rate than price rises.
8) Is a fall in the value of the pound better for importers or exporters?
9) Give one scenario where a business would expect no competition.
10) Give three potential benefits of high unemployment for businesses.

Total:

Quiz 4 Date: ...... / ...... / ......

1) What is meant by a competitive market?
2) True or false? Only the global economy affects exchange rates.
3) Give one way a firm can check its marketing mix is right for its products.
4) Explain why lots of competition may result in lower profits for a business.
5) Give two disadvantages of globalisation for businesses.
6) Explain how high unemployment can lead to businesses' sales falling.
7) Explain why the health of the economy can cause uncertainty for all businesses.
8) Outline what a business in a competitive market may do to show that their product is better than their rivals.
9) How does a higher interest rate affect spending?
10) Explain how firms that export from the UK could benefit when the value of the pound falls.

Total:

Section 3 — Business Operations

Supply Chains

First Go:
...../...../.....

Supply Chain Basics

SUPPLY CHAIN — the group of firms that are involved in the .... required to make a .... product or .... available to the customer.

The supply chain will .... depending on the product or ...., but will typically be:

supplier of ....

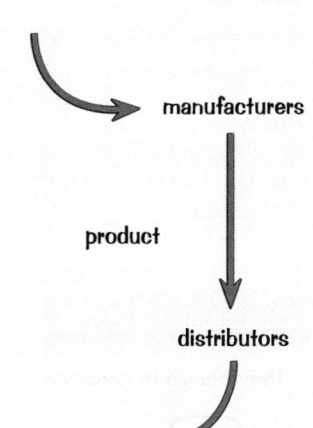

→ manufacturers

.... product

↓

distributors

↩

Distributor — buys products from a .... and sells them to .... and ....
.... — sells products directly to consumers.

All .... of a supply chain need to be ....

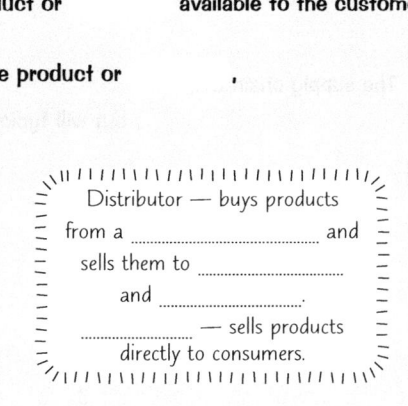

Choosing a Supplier

Three things to consider:

① Cost
Cheaper suppliers might have .... products. It might be better to .... more to get, e.g. better .... products or faster ....

② Quality
Quality needs to be .... Customers may blame .... over .... for poor quality products and choose to ....

③ Reliability
.... from suppliers should be reliable — goods should arrive .... and be ....

Second Go: ..... / ..... / .....

Supply Chains

Supply Chain Basics

SUPPLY CHAIN — the group of firms that

The supply chain will   , but will typically be:

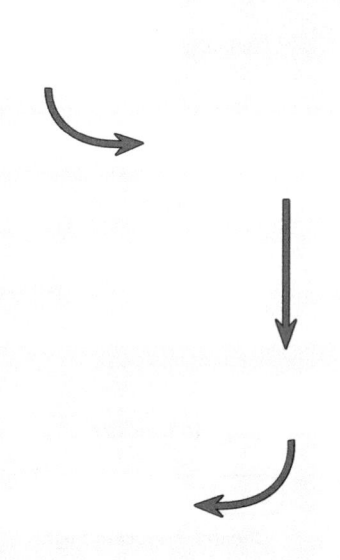

Distributor — ....
....
....
Retailer — ....
....

All members of a

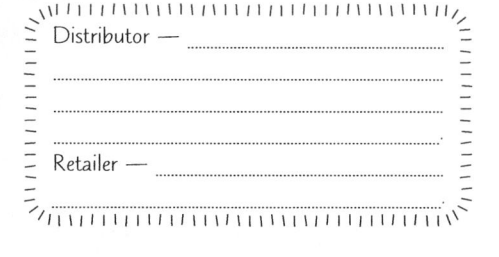

Choosing a Supplier

Three things to consider:

1 (Cost)

Cheaper suppliers might

It might be better to

2 (Quality)

Quality needs

Customers may

3 (...............)

Delivery from

Section 3 — Business Operations

More on Supply Chains

First Go: ...../...../.....

Procurement and Logistics

PROCUREMENT — _____ and _____ things that a firm _____ needs from suppliers _____ of the firm.

LOGISTICS — getting _____ or _____ from one part of the _____ to another.

Two benefits of effective procurement and logistics systems:

1) Improved efficiency
- The business gets the _____ it needs at the right _____.
- This means there are no breaks in _____ and no _____ are wasted.

2) Reduced costs
- The business gets _____ at the best _____ (so _____ is not wasted).
- This reduces _____, so the firm can make more _____ on each item, or reduce _____.

Three Reasons for Managing a Supply Chain Effectively

1) Develops good _____

Businesses that work _____ with _____ can carry out processes in _____ and _____ ways.

2) Gets the best _____ and _____

There can be many suppliers for a business to _____. Businesses that _____ suppliers can get the best _____ and _____ for the _____ they need.

3) Reduces _____ and unnecessary _____

Businesses should reduce _____ and cut unnecessary _____ in their supply chain. This helps to make the business more _____ and have _____ production times.

Section 3 — Business Operations

More on Supply Chains

Second Go: ...../...../......

Procurement and Logistics

PROCUREMENT —

LOGISTICS —

Two benefits of effective procurement and logistics systems:

1) Improved ....
- The business gets
- This means there are

2) Reduced ....
- The business gets

- This reduces

Three Reasons for Managing a Supply Chain Effectively

1) Develops good relationships

Businesses that

2) Gets the best price and value

There can be

Businesses that

3) Reduces waste and unnecessary costs

Businesses should reduce

This helps to

Section 3 — Business Operations

Production and Efficiency

First Go: ..... / ..... / .....

Job Production

JOB PRODUCTION — each _____ has a _____ based on the customer's _____ .

➕ • Unique, _____ products — customers are _____ to pay a _____ , which can lead to _____ .

➖ • High _____ costs for _____ workers.
• Often _____ and _____ .

Flow Production

FLOW PRODUCTION — _____ are _____ and made as _____ as possible. Production is _____ .

➕ • Gain from _____ — low _____ means _____ , _____ prices.
• High _____ .

➖ • _____ — lots of _____ is needed initially, e.g. to buy _____ .
• Lots of _____ usually needed, e.g. to _____ products.

Lean Production

LEAN PRODUCTION — the business _____ to use as few _____ and _____ to have as _____ as possible.

JUST-IN-TIME (JIT) — a form of _____ production where _____ are made just in time for _____ to customers.

② **JUST-IN-CASE (JIC)** — _____ stocks are kept at every _____ of the _____ in case of a supply _____ or an increase in customer demand.

➕ Production can continue if there's a _____ with _____ of _____ .

➖ Can be _____ storing _____ .

Two Ways to Manage Stock

① **JUST-IN-TIME (JIT)** — _____ levels are kept at a _____ .

➕ Less _____ spent _____ stock, e.g. on warehouse _____ and _____ .

➖ • More _____ for _____ stock _____ .
• Less gain from _____ — stock isn't bought in _____ .

> 'Stock' can mean any _____ that's needed in production or _____ , e.g. raw materials or a _____ .

Section 3 — Business Operations

Production and Efficiency

Second Go: ..... /..... /.....

Job Production

JOB PRODUCTION —

+ Unique, high-quality products —

−
-
- Often

Flow Production

FLOW PRODUCTION —

+
- Gain from

-

−
- Capital-intensive —

- Lots of

Lean Production

LEAN PRODUCTION —

JUST-IN-TIME (JIT) —

② JUST-IN-CASE (JIC) —

+ Production can

− Can be

Two Ways to Manage Stock

① JUST-IN-TIME (JIT) —

+ Less money spent

−
- More cost for
- Less gain from

'Stock' can mean ....
....
....
e.g. ....
....

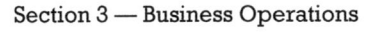

Section 3 — Business Operations

Mixed Practice Quizzes

Here's a job for you — try these questions covering p.59-64 to see if you're really in the flow. Mark each quiz yourself to check how well you're doing.

Quiz 1   Date: ...... / ...... / ......

1) What is flow production?
2) What term describes finding and buying things that a firm needs from suppliers outside of the firm?
3) Give two disadvantages of using just-in-time to manage stock.
4) True or false? All members of a supply chain need to be dependable.
5) What is meant by 'stock'?
6) Why might using job production lead to high labour costs?
7) Explain why it is important to consider reliability when choosing a supplier.
8) What is the just-in-case method of managing stock?
9) Outline why a business should reduce waste and unnecessary costs in their supply chain.
10) Which method of production gains from economies of scale?

Total:

Quiz 2   Date: ...... / ...... / ......

1) What is meant by 'procurement'?
2) Explain why it is important to consider cost when choosing a supplier.
3) What method of production is used to make individual products with a unique design based on a customer's specification?
4) Give two benefits of having effective procurement and logistics systems.
5) What is just-in-time production?
6) How can businesses ensure they get the best price and value for the goods they need?
7) Give two disadvantages of using flow production.
8) Which type of firm is at the start of a supply chain?
9) Give one advantage of using job production.
10) Give three reasons for managing a supply chain effectively.

Total:

Mixed Practice Quizzes

Quiz 3 Date: ...... / ...... / ......

1) Explain why a firm should consider quality when choosing a supplier.
2) What is meant by 'logistics'?
3) Give one advantage of using just-in-time stock management.
4) Outline the difference between a distributor and a retailer.
5) Which method of production has high productivity — job production or flow production?
6) How might effective procurement and logistics improve a firm's efficiency?
7) True or false? A supply chain will vary depending on the product or service.
8) Outline what is meant by 'lean production'.
9) Who is typically involved in the supply chain immediately after the manufacturing of a product?
10) State one disadvantage of using just-in-case to manage stock.

Total:

Quiz 4 Date: ...... / ...... / ......

1) What is meant by 'supply chain'?
2) Give one advantage of using just-in-case to manage stock.
3) True or false? Using flow production requires minimal storage space.
4) Name three types of firm involved in a typical supply chain.
5) What is the benefit to businesses of working closely with suppliers?
6) Explain how effective procurement and logistics systems can reduce costs.
7) What method of managing stock keeps levels at a bare minimum?
8) Give three things a firm should consider when choosing a supplier.
9) Give two disadvantages of using job production.
10) True or false? 'Just-in-time' is an example of lean production.

Total:

Quality

First Go: ...../...../.....

Customer Expectations

Customers expect quality from all parts of a business:

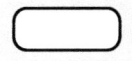

[ ]
- Customers _____ products to be of _____.
- They should _____ properly and not _____.

Services
- Services should be _____ of _____.
- Customers also expect a _____ of _____.

Three Benefits of Maintaining Quality

1. **Higher price**
   Customers will often pay a _____ price for _____ products.

2. **Increased sales**
   Customers who are _____ with quality are more likely to make repeat _____, which increases _____.

3. **Better reputation**
   Businesses that provide _____ products will have a better _____ and _____.
   They'll gain _____ customers and _____ customers are likely to use the _____ again.

Two Costs of Maintaining Quality

1. **Staff training**
   Staff need to be _____ do their job properly to _____ high quality _____.
   Staff training costs _____ and _____.

2. **Inspection**
   Products need to be _____ to _____ their quality.
   This costs _____ and _____.

Two Costs of Not Maintaining Quality

1. _____ of services
   A _____ in quality can _____ the services that a business _____.
   This can mean a _____.

2. **Product** _____
   Unsafe products are _____.
   A _____ or _____ would need to be _____.
   This can be _____ and can affect the firm's _____.

Section 3 — Business Operations

Second Go: ..... /..... /.....

Quality

Customer Expectations

Customers expect quality from all parts of a business:

☐

- Customers expect
- They should

☐

-
- Customers also expect

Three Benefits of Maintaining Quality

1) .... price
Customers will often

2) .... sales
Customers who are

3) .... reputation
Businesses that

They'll gain

Two Costs of Maintaining Quality

1) Staff training
Staff need to

Staff training

2) Inspection
Products need to

This

Two Costs of Not Maintaining Quality

1) Disrupted provision of services
A drop in

This can mean

2) Product recalls
Unsafe
A refund or

This can be

Section 3 — Business Operations

Quality Management

First Go: ...../...../......

Quality Checks

Firms check quality to find .... before products reach the .... Firms usually check:

A firm needs to decide what .... is .... to them.

.... from suppliers. → Random .... of work in .... → Random .... of .... products.

Quality checks can be .... , but still less .... than customers .... items or not .... from the firm again.

Three Ways to Measure Quality

1. Test the .... properties (e.g. .... and ....) match the exact ....

2. Monitor how many .... and customer .... there are.

   The firm can decide what .... or .... it's .... comfortable with.

3. Do customer .... to assess how .... customers are.

Total Quality Management (TQM)

TOTAL QUALITY MANAGEMENT — a .... that aims to make every .... in a firm .... for quality to ensure that it remains ....

The focus is on:

Getting things right ....
This reduces .... by reducing ....

Increasing customer .... — emphasis is put on the quality of .... and .... service.

Maintaining Quality with Growth

.... business .... quickly → output of .... to .... needs → more .... quickly .... quality → .... to keep .... high

- It may become .... to .... all the necessary quality ....
- .... may be cut to make products ....
- More .... may be needed — but it takes time to .... new ....

A growing business might:

become a .... — but keeping high quality across the .... can involve a lot of staff training and regular ....

.... some tasks — but it can be .... to .... to a firm that delivers high quality (and using a .... firm can lead to a fall in quality).

Section 3 — Business Operations

Quality Management

Second Go: ..... /..... /.....

Quality Checks

Firms check quality to

Firms usually check:

→

Quality checks can be

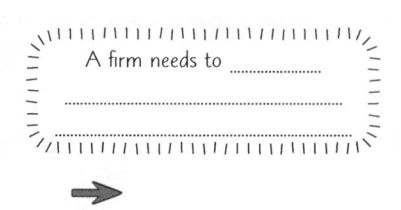

A firm needs to ....

→

Three Ways to Measure Quality

1. Test the

2. Monitor how many

The firm can decide ....

3. Do customer surveys to

Total Quality Management (TQM)

TOTAL QUALITY MANAGEMENT —

The focus is on:

Increasing customer satisfaction —

Maintaining Quality with Growth

business → output of products → more difficult to

- It may become hard to
- Corners may be
- More employees may be

A growing business might:

become a franchisor — but keeping   outsource some tasks — but it can be

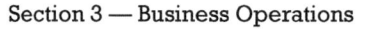

Section 3 — Business Operations

Customer Service

First Go:
...../...../.....

Providing Customer Service

CUSTOMER SERVICE — any _____ a business has with its _____ .

Firms should _____ great customer service throughout the _____ .

Three Ways of Providing Good Customer Service

1 Have excellent product _____

- Questions are answered _____ and _____ .
- Customer gets product most _____ to their _____ .
- Customer feels _____ buying from the firm.

2 _____ well with customers

- Staff should be _____ , _____ , listen to _____ and create a positive _____ .
- Makes customer feel _____ and _____ .
- Have _____ of making the _____ positive, e.g. free _____ or _____ delivery.

3 Offer _____ service

- Offer _____ to customer on how to _____ product.
- Have a post-sales _____ where staff can help to resolve any _____ .
- Offer _____ for products that _____ it. E.g. cars and boilers.

Six Stages of the Sales Process

1 Finding _____

2 Approaching the _____

3 Assessing their _____

4 Presenting _____ to them

5 _____ (customer agrees to _____)

6 _____

Second Go: ..... /..... /.....

Customer Service

Providing Customer Service

CUSTOMER SERVICE —

Firms should provide

Three Ways of Providing Good Customer Service

1 Have excellent ....
-
- Customer gets
- Customer feels

2 .... with customers
- Staff should be

-
- Have

3 Offer ....
- Offer

- Have a

- Offer servicing

E.g. cars and boilers.

Six Stages of the Sales Process

1
2
3
4
5
6

Section 3 — Business Operations

More on Customer Service

First Go: ...../...../.....

Advances in Technology

Many customers now have _____ to the _____ and choose to do things _____.

This has changed how firms provide _____.

Websites and E-commerce

E-commerce is _____ and _____ products using the _____.

Websites can be used for e-commerce and providing good _____.

Websites:
- allow _____ ordering.
- provide ways of _____ the firm.
- allow _____ to services via _____.

Social Media

Social media allows communication _____ and the _____ of content _____.

Social media can be used:
- by firms to _____ with customers (e.g. to show them _____ a product).
- by _____ to contact a firm (e.g. with _____ or complaints).

> For many firms, providing good _____ increases _____, so the benefit _____ the cost.

Importance of Good Customer Service

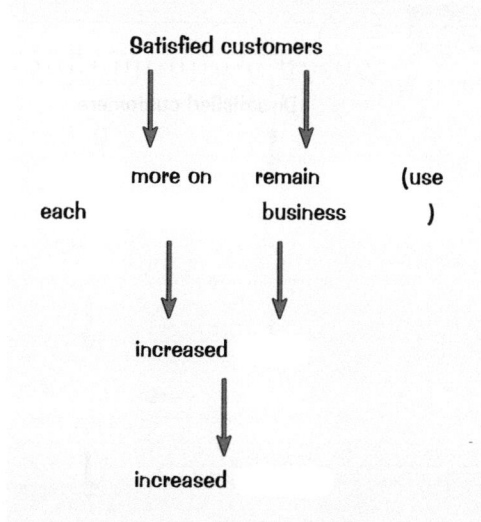

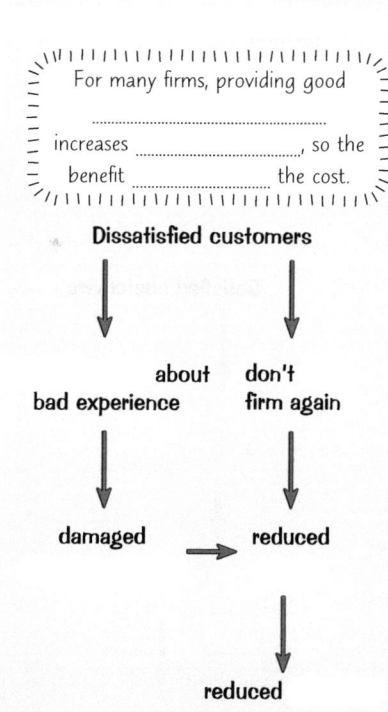

Satisfied customers
- _____ each _____
- more on _____
- remain _____ business
- (use _____)

↓
increased _____
↓
increased _____

Dissatisfied customers
- _____ about bad experience
- don't _____ firm again

↓
damaged _____ → reduced _____
↓
reduced _____

Section 3 — Business Operations

Second Go: ..... / ..... / .....

More on Customer Service

Advances in Technology

Many customers

This has

Websites and E-commerce

E-commerce is

Websites can be

Websites:
- allow
- provide

- allow

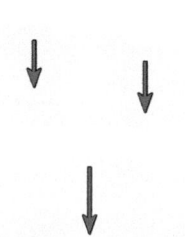

Social Media

Social media allows

Social media can be used:
- by firms to

- by customers to

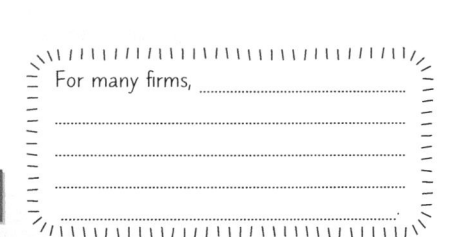

> For many firms, ...
> ....
> ....
> ....

Importance of Good Customer Service

Satisfied customers

↓   ↓

↓   ↓

↓

Dissatisfied customers

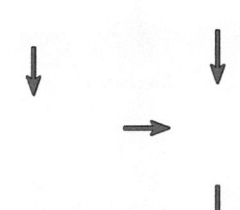

↓   ↓

↓   ↓
    →

↓

Section 3 — Business Operations

Mixed Practice Quizzes

Here's another set of questions, this time about p.67-74, to assess the quality of your business knowledge. Mark each quiz and find your total score.

Quiz 1 — Date: ...... / ...... / ......

1) Outline the quality that customers expect for the goods they buy.
2) What is customer service?
3) Give three stages during production when firms will perform quality checks.
4) Give one way firms use social media to provide customer service.
5) Explain how having to recall a product would affect a firm.
6) How might having customers satisfied with quality increase the sales of a firm?
7) Give three reasons why it can be difficult to maintain quality standards when a business grows quickly.
8) What is the first stage of the sales process?
9) True or false? One way to measure the quality of a product is to monitor customer complaints.
10) Give three benefits to a customer of using a firm's website.

Total:

Quiz 2 — Date: ...... / ...... / ......

1) How has technology changed the way firms provide customer service?
2) Give three benefits to a firm of maintaining quality.
3) In the sales process, what is meant by 'closing'?
4) What is meant by 'total quality management'?
5) Outline how staff can make a customer feel important and valued.
6) Describe why a firm might avoid outsourcing tasks.
7) Outline the effects on a firm of having dissatisfied customers.
8) True or false? Customers are often willing to pay higher prices for better quality products.
9) State three ways a firm can provide good customer service.
10) Why is it worthwhile for firms to spend money on quality checks?

Total:

Mixed Practice Quizzes

Quiz 3 — Date: ...... / ...... / ......

1) Describe how a customer benefits from staff that have excellent product knowledge.
2) How can social media be used by customers to communicate with firms?
3) Why do firms carry out quality checks?
4) True or false? Great customer service is only needed after the sales process.
5) Give two costs to a business of maintaining quality.
6) Suggest why firms provide good customer service even though it is costly.
7) Give two actions a growing business might take that makes it difficult to maintain quality.
8) Suggest three ways that a firm can provide post-sales service.
9) Give one focus of a firm when using total quality management.
10) Explain how high quality leads to new customers for a business.

Total:

Quiz 4 — Date: ...... / ...... / ......

1) Give the six stages of the sales process.
2) Give one disadvantage to a firm of training its staff.
3) What is the term used to describe buying and selling on the internet?
4) Describe three ways to measure the quality of a product.
5) Give one way that a firm could provide a more positive customer experience through its delivery service.
6) True or false? All firms have the same level of quality that is acceptable to them.
7) How could a dissatisfied customer damage the brand image of a firm?
8) Explain why it is difficult to maintain high quality standards across franchises.
9) Outline the effects on a firm of having satisfied customers.
10) Give two costs to a business of not maintaining quality.

Total:

Section 3 — Business Operations

Section 4 — Human Resources

Internal Organisational Structures

First Go: ..... / ..... / .....

Four Layers within a Hierarchy

Reasons for internal organisational structures:

- individual   are
- a   exists for every activity

1. ———— — responsible for the business's   .
2. MANAGERS — organise   the strategy.
3. ———— — look after specific   or small teams of operatives.
4. OPERATIVES — given   by supervisors or   .

At each level some   is   to the level   .

         OF CONTROL — number of workers   to one   .

         OF COMMAND — chain connecting   to operatives.

Fast communication —   layers of management:

- ———— to pass on one message to
- Hard for managers to talk to each worker

Tall Organisational Structure

- ———— chain of command
- ———— layers of management
- Managers have   span of control

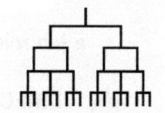

⬇

Workers can be

⬇

Firm is more

Communication can be   and   :

- ———— passing the message along chain of command.
- ———— communication is hard if lots of managers need to be involved.

Flat Organisational Structure

- ———— chain of command
- Managers have a   span of control

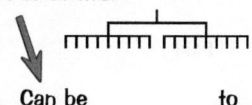

⬇

- Can be   to effectively manage a   of employees at once   .

i.e. firm removes layers of _____.

Changing Organisational Structures

         firms have   structures, often run by just the   .

Firm grows ➡

1. Employs more _____.
2. Employs _____ to organise workforce.
3. Structure gets _____.

➡ Firm _____ to avoid becoming too tall.

Second Go: ..... /..... /.....

Internal Organisational Structures

Four Layers within a Hierarchy

Reasons for internal organisational structures:
- individual

- a job role

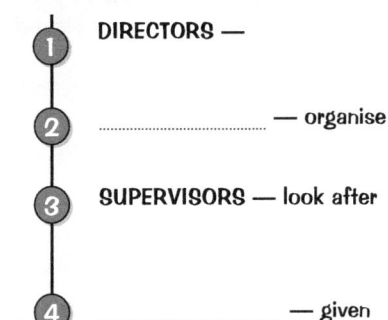

1. DIRECTORS —
2. .... — organise
3. SUPERVISORS — look after
4. .... — given

At each level

SPAN OF CONTROL —

CHAIN OF COMMAND —

Fast

- Easy to
- Hard for

Tall Organisational Structure

- Long
- More
- Managers

⬇

Workers can be

⬇

Firm

Communication can be .... and .... :
- Lots of people

- Verbal communication

Flat Organisational Structure

- Short
- Managers

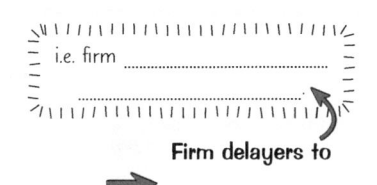

↘ Can be difficult

Changing Organisational Structures

Small firms have

Firm → grows

1. Employs
2. Employs
3. Structure

i.e. firm ....
....

→ Firm delayers to

Section 4 — Human Resources

More on Organisational Structures

First Go: ...../...../.....

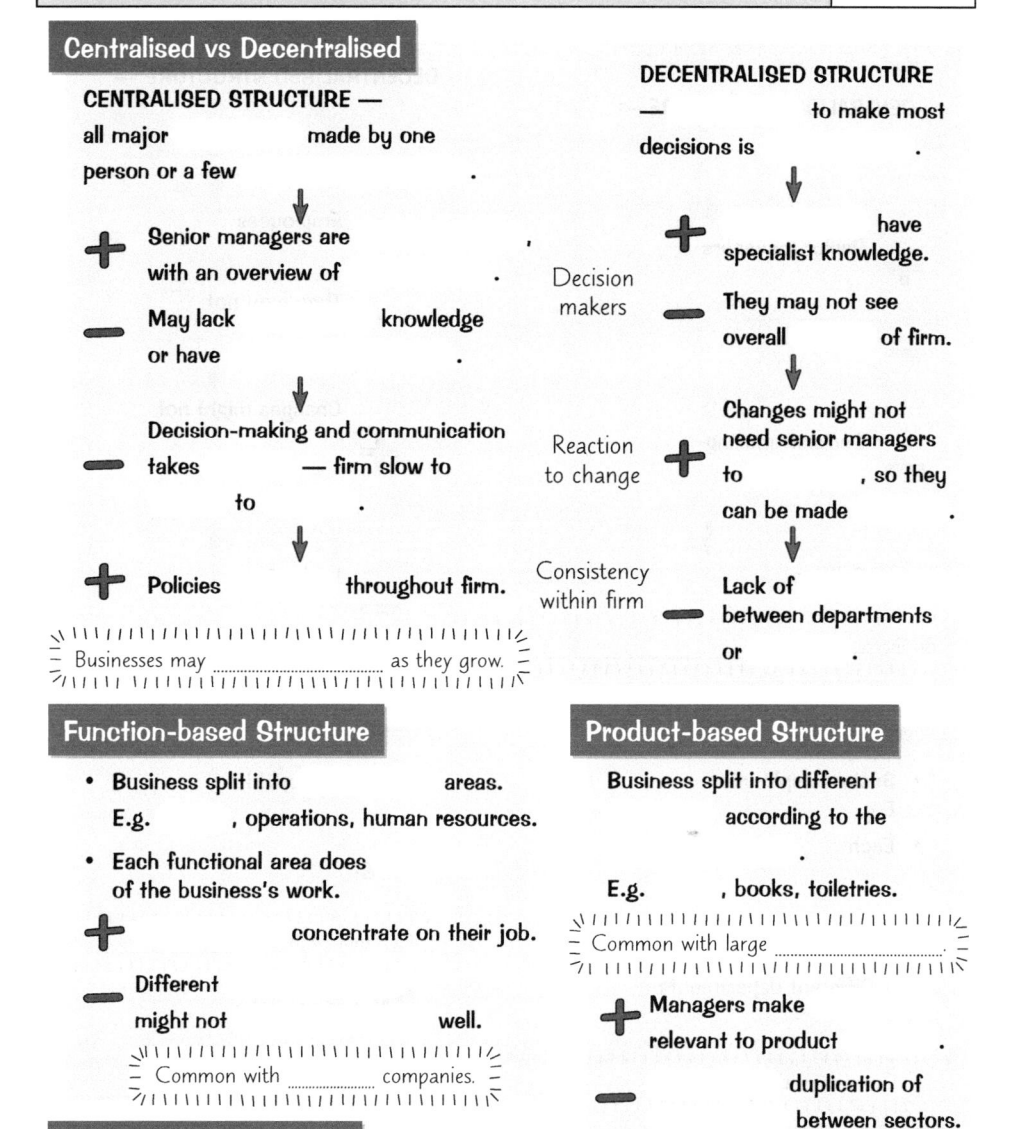

Centralised vs Decentralised

CENTRALISED STRUCTURE —
all major _____ made by one person or a few _____.

➡️

+ Senior managers are _____, with an overview of _____.

− May lack _____ knowledge or have _____.

➡️

− Decision-making and communication takes _____ — firm slow to _____ to _____.

➡️

+ Policies _____ throughout firm.

Businesses may _____ as they grow.

DECENTRALISED STRUCTURE —
_____ to make most decisions is _____.

➡️

+ _____ have specialist knowledge.

− They may not see overall _____ of firm.

➡️

+ Changes might not need senior managers to _____, so they can be made _____.

➡️

− Lack of _____ between departments or _____.

Decision makers

Reaction to change

Consistency within firm

Function-based Structure

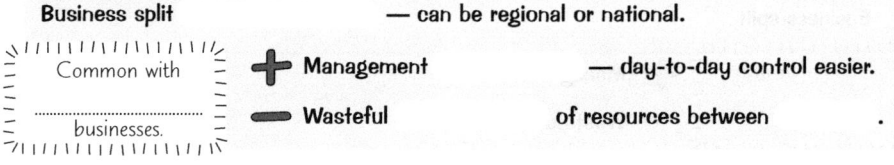

- Business split into _____ areas.
  E.g. _____, operations, human resources.
- Each functional area does _____ of the business's work.

+ _____ concentrate on their job.

− Different _____ might not _____ well.

Common with _____ companies.

Product-based Structure

Business split into different _____ according to the _____.

E.g. _____, books, toiletries.

Common with large _____.

+ Managers make _____ relevant to product _____.

− _____ duplication of _____ between sectors.

Region-based Structure

Business split _____ — can be regional or national.

Common with _____ businesses.

+ Management _____ — day-to-day control easier.

− Wasteful _____ of resources between _____.

Section 4 — Human Resources

Second Go: ..... / ..... / .....

More on Organisational Structures

Centralised vs Decentralised

CENTRALISED STRUCTURE —

↓
+ Senior managers
− May lack
↓
− Decision-making
↓
+ Policies

Businesses may _____.

DECENTRALISED STRUCTURE —

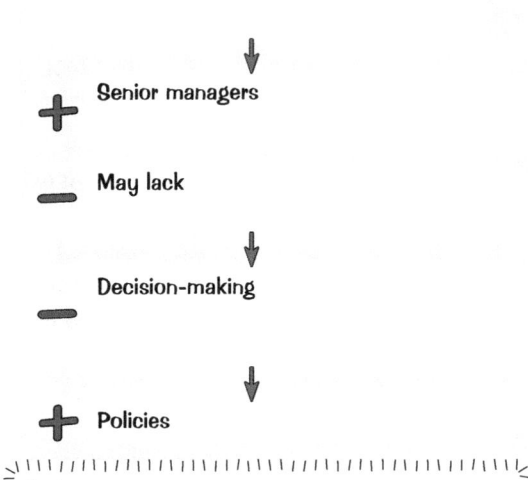

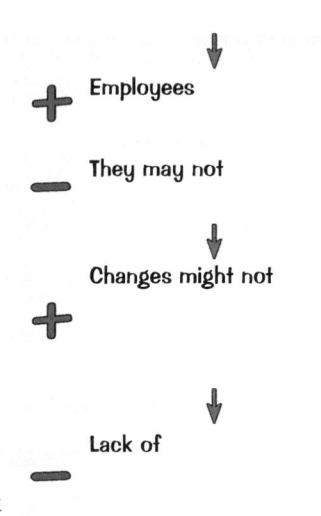

↓
+ Employees
− They may not
↓
+ Changes might not
↓
− Lack of

Function-based Structure

- Business split into
  E.g.
- Each

+ Specialists
− Different departments

Common with _____.

Product-based Structure

Business split into

E.g.

Common with large _____.

+ Managers make

− Wasteful

Region-based Structure

Business split

Common with _____ businesses.

+ Management
− Wasteful

Section 4 — Human Resources

Contracts of Employment

First Go: ..... / ..... / .....

Information in Contracts

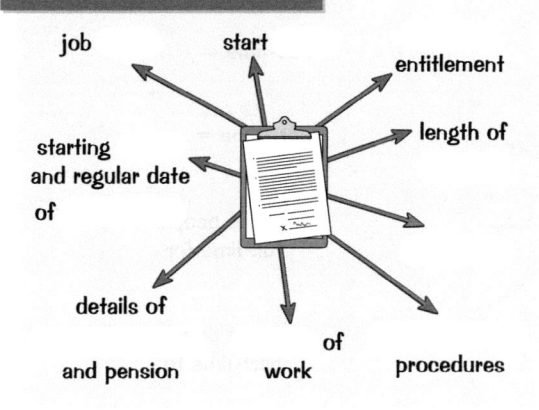

- job
- start
- entitlement
- length of
- starting and regular date of
- details of _____ and pension
- _____ of work
- _____ procedures

Full-Time vs Part-Time

Full-time = about _____ hours a week.

Part-time = between _____ hours a week.

- Some people work full-time for _____ reasons.

- Some people work _____ to spend extra time with _____.

Advantages of full-time employees	Advantages of part-time employees
Employees likely have only _____ — so firms have more _____ over when they work.	• Employees often _____ with hours and can fill in for _____ staff. • Good for firms that are only _____ at _____.

Job Shares

_____ employees share the work and pay of _____.

➕ **Advantages**
- Employees can work extra _____ if the other is _____ — _____ still gets done.
- Employees bring different _____ to the job.
- Good for employees who want to work _____ hours.

For job shares to work, each employee's .... must be clear and there must be good ....

Zero Hour Contracts

A zero hour contract means:
- employer doesn't have to _____ any work
- _____ doesn't have to accept any work

Used in businesses with lots of _____ in _____.

➕ Firms don't _____ paying staff when they aren't _____ — cheap form of _____.

➕ Good for people who want to earn _____ but also turn work down if they're _____.

➖ Can be hard for people who _____ on the work to earn a _____.

Section 4 — Human Resources

Second Go:
..... / ..... / .....

Contracts of Employment

Information in Contracts

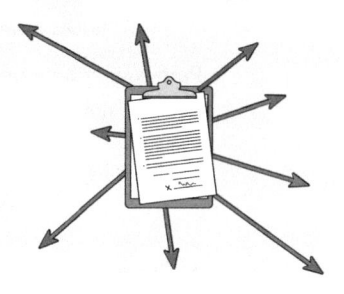

Full-Time vs Part-Time

Full-time =

Part-time =

- Some people work full-time for

- Some people work part-time to

Advantages of full-time employees	Advantages of part-time employees
Employees likely	• Employees often flexible
	• Good for firms that

Job Shares

Two employees

+ Advantages

- Employees can

- Employees bring

- Good for

For job shares to work, ...

Zero Hour Contracts

A zero hour contract means:
- employer
- employee

Used in businesses

+ Firms don't waste

+ Good for people who

− Can be hard for

Section 4 — Human Resources

Mixed Practice Quizzes

See if you've organised your revision properly by having a go at these quizzes that test p.77-82. Mark them yourself and work out your score.

Quiz 1 — Date: ...... / ...... / ......

1) What is meant by 'chain of command'?
2) How many hours does a full-time employee usually work each week?
3) Describe two disadvantages of a centralised organisational structure.
4) What is meant by 'delayering'?
5) State three examples of functional areas in a firm with a function-based structure.
6) What type of contract is used in firms with lots of fluctuations in demand?
7) Give two impacts of having a tall organisational structure on communication in a firm.
8) True or false? At each level of the hierarchy in a firm, some responsibility is delegated to the level below.
9) Give one advantage to a firm of having part-time employees.
10) Explain why a firm's structure might become taller as it grows.

Total:

Quiz 2 — Date: ...... / ...... / ......

1) What role is responsible for deciding on a business's strategy?
2) List five things that are included in a contract of employment.
3) Describe one advantage to a firm of employing full-time workers.
4) True or false? Tall structures have a short chain of command.
5) Describe two advantages of a decentralised organisational structure.
6) Give one advantage and one disadvantage of a product-based structure.
7) What is meant by 'span of control'?
8) What term describes a contract where employers don't have to offer any work and employees don't have to accept any work?
9) Give one disadvantage of using a region-based structure.
10) Is communication fast or slow in a flat organisational structure?

Total:

Section 4 — Human Resources

Mixed Practice Quizzes

Quiz 3 Date: ...... / ...... / ......

1) Describe the role of a manager in a business.
2) Give two advantages to a firm of using job shares.
3) What is a centralised organisational structure?
4) True or false? Managers with a wide span of control can easily manage lots of employees at once.
5) Which role within a hierarchy is given tasks by supervisors or managers?
6) Why might someone choose to work part-time?
7) Which type of organisational structure has a long chain of command?
8) Explain one disadvantage of a tall organisational structure.
9) Give one advantage of a firm having a region-based structure.
10) List two advantages of zero hour contracts.

Total:

Quiz 4 Date: ...... / ...... / ......

1) In what type of organisational structure is the authority to make most decisions shared out?
2) How many hours does a part-time employee usually work each week?
3) Explain why a narrow span of control is a disadvantage of a tall organisational structure.
4) Give two reasons why businesses have internal organisational structures.
5) True or false? Businesses always keep a centralised structure as they grow.
6) Outline two things that are needed for a job share to work.
7) Which role in an organisational structure typically looks after specific projects or small teams?
8) Give two advantages of a centralised organisational structure.
9) Where would an employee find details of their holiday entitlement?
10) What is meant by a 'product-based structure'?

Total:

Section 4 — Human Resources

Recruitment

First Go: ..... / ..... / .....

Two Features of Job Adverts

JOB ANALYSIS — .... in which every little .... of a job is thought about.
This is used to create a job advert which includes:

1. **JOB DESCRIPTION** — written description of what a ....

   Includes: job title, ..., duties, who job holder reports to, ...

2. **PERSON SPECIFICATION** — list of qualifications, ..., experience and .... needed for a job.

Internal Recruitment

INTERNAL RECRUITMENT — .... employees are recruited into .... within a business.
Job advertised .... the business.

+ • .... to recruit
  • posts filled ....
  • candidates already .... firm, already know candidates

− • fewer new ....
  • candidate's .... role must be filled

Selection Process

Written Application
- Curriculum vitae (CV) — .... about the candidate and their skills or ....
- .... form — all the info the firm needs and nothing else.

References
- .... line manager provides statement about candidate's ....

External Recruitment

EXTERNAL RECRUITMENT — people from .... the .... are recruited.
Job advertised ....

+ • advert seen by .... people — more .... to find right candidate

−

Four Benefits of Good Recruitment

1. right skills and .... → minimal training → .... productivity
2. best .... → high quality ....
3. .... to .... role and enjoying job → good customer ....
4. well-suited to .... → less likely to .... → good staff ....

Interviews
- Same questions for ....
- Assess ...., skills, general attitude.
- Skills for a good interview are not always .... to job.

Tests
- Might test ...., potential, personal qualities, ...
- Assess .... relevant to job.

Section 4 — Human Resources

Recruitment

Second Go: ...../...../.....

Two Features of Job Adverts

JOB ANALYSIS —

This is used to create a job advert which includes:

1. **JOB DESCRIPTION —**

2. **PERSON SPECIFICATION —**

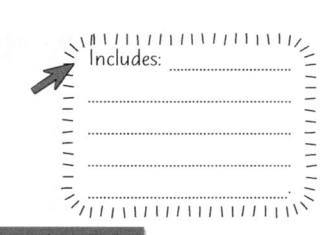

Includes: ....
....
....
....
....

Internal Recruitment

INTERNAL RECRUITMENT —

Job advertised

+
- cheaper
- posts
- candidates already

−
- fewer
- candidate's previous

External Recruitment

EXTERNAL RECRUITMENT —

Job advertised

+ advert seen

−

Four Benefits of Good Recruitment

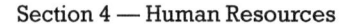

1. right .... → minimal .... → .... productivity
2. .... → high ....
3. .... to role → good ....
   and ....
4. .... → less .... → good ....

Selection Process

Written Application
- Curriculum vitae (CV) —
- Application form —

References
- Previous

Interviews
- Same questions
- Assess
- Skills for

Tests
- Might test
- Assess

Section 4 — Human Resources

Staff Training

First Go: ...../...../.....

Induction Training

Induction training introduces a .... to their workplace and helps them .... It includes:

- .... them to other workers
- explaining .... and procedures
- initial .... on their job

Advantages
- New employees feel ....
- They are .... likely to make .... — so they become .... quickly.
- They feel welcome and .... — so they're less likely to ....

On-the-Job Training

Employee learns by .... by more experienced .... how to do their job and then ....

Most suitable for learning .... skills when it's .... and ....

On-the-job training is the .... type.

+ Cost .... — employee works and learns at the same ....

− Training given by .... — bad working practices can be ....

− More .... than on-the-job.

Off-the-Job Training

Employee learns .... from their workplace — e.g. at a local ....

Most suitable for learning .... information, such as skills not related to a ....

+ High .... — taught by people .... to train others.

Benefits of Training

+ Trained staff are better at their jobs → More efficient and ....

↓ ↓
Produce higher .... goods   Provide better ....

+ Staff stay up to date with .... in ....

+ Employees are more ....
   ↘ Better staff ....

Section 4 — Human Resources

Second Go: ...../...../.....

Staff Training

Induction Training

Induction training

It includes:
- introducing
- explaining

- initial

+ Advantages
- New employees
- They are less likely to

- They feel welcome

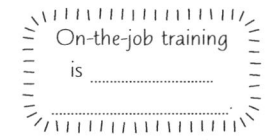

On-the-Job Training

Employee learns

Most suitable for

+ Cost effective —

− Training given

− More

On-the-job training is ....

Off-the-Job Training

Employee learns

Most suitable for

+ High quality —

Benefits of Training

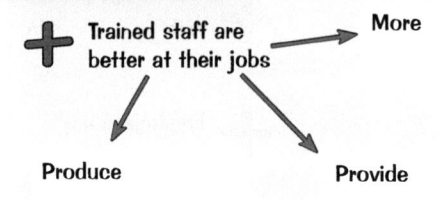

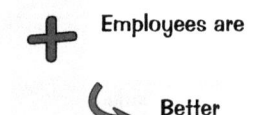

+ Trained staff are better at their jobs → More

↓ Produce

↘ Provide

+ Staff stay

+ Employees are

↳ Better

Section 4 — Human Resources

Financial Motivation

First Go: ..... /..... /.....

Effect of Motivation

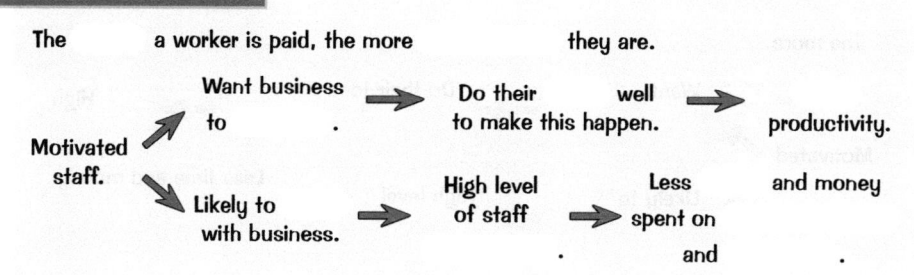

The _____ a worker is paid, the more _____ they are.

Motivated staff.
→ Want business to _____ . → Do their _____ well to make this happen. → _____ productivity.
→ Likely to _____ with business. → High level of _____ staff → Less _____ spent on _____ and _____ . → _____ and money _____ .

Wages

- Paid _____ or _____ .
- Common for _____ workers.

Time Rate — workers paid according to _____ .
Best when measuring output is _____ — e.g. driving a bus.

➕ Encourages people to work _____ .
➖ Encourages people to work _____ .

Piece Rate — workers paid according to _____ .
Best when measuring output is _____ — e.g. sewing garments.

➕ Encourages people to work _____ .
➖ Working too quickly can reduce _____ .

Salary

- A _____ paid every _____ .
- It doesn't _____ — even if the number of _____ worked changes.
- Usually paid to _____ staff who don't _____ help make the product.

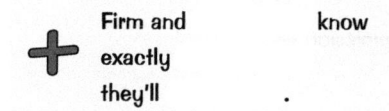

➕ Firm and _____ know exactly _____ they'll _____ .
➖ Pay not linked to _____ — doesn't _____ employees to work _____ .

Extra Payments

Some firms offer _____ incentives — on top of the _____ wage or salary.

_____ — paid to _____ staff for every item they _____ .

Profit _____ schemes — e.g. where a _____ of firm's profit is _____ between _____ .

Section 4 — Human Resources

Second Go: ..... /..... /.....

Financial Motivation

Effect of Motivation

The more

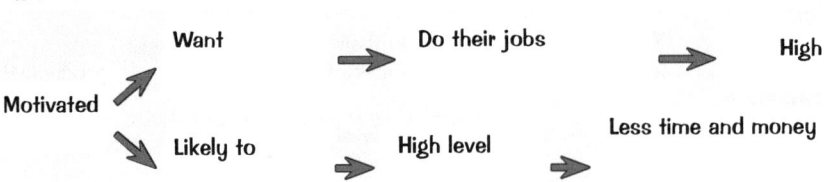

Motivated → Want → Do their jobs → High

Motivated → Likely to → High level → Less time and money

Wages

- Paid
- Common

Time Rate —

Best when

+ Encourages

− Encourages

Piece Rate —

Best when

+ Encourages

− Working too quickly

Salary

- A fixed
- It doesn't change
- Usually paid

+ Firm and workers

− Pay not linked

Extra Payments

Some firms offer

Commission —

Profit sharing schemes —

Section 4 — Human Resources

Non-Financial Motivation

First Go: ...../...../.....

Training

___ and skills up to date. → Job performed ___ . → Increased ___ and job satisfaction. → ___ motivated.

Learning ___ means employees can take on new ___ and greater ___ .

Employees ___ and ___ with the firm. ↙ ↘ Potential for ___ boosts ___ further.

Four Management Styles

① ___ (or autocratic) managers make decisions ___ without ___ staff.

② Paternalistic managers make decisions ___ , but after ___ with workers.

③ ___ managers allow workforce some ___ over decisions.

④ ___ managers allow workers to perform tasks as they ___ — offering ___ as needed.

+ ___ management is effective at handling ___ .

Can ___ staff if they feel their views are ___ .

A ___ of management styles is often used — depending on the ___ .

Workers have ___ into ___ .
↓
They feel ___ and ___ with work.
↓
They are more ___ .

Fringe Benefits

FRINGE BENEFIT — any ___ that is not part of a worker's ___ .

Might include:
- staff ___ on firm's products
- use of ___
- ___ membership
- ___ meal
- health ___

These cost money for the ___ and they ___ save money for the ___ .

☹ ✓   😐 ✓   🙂 ✓

Section 4 — Human Resources

Second Go: ...../...../.....

Non-Financial Motivation

Training

Knowledge → Job → Increased → More

Learning new skills

Employees less bored ↙   ↘ Potential for

Four Management Styles

1. Authoritarian (or ....) managers

2. Paternalistic managers

3. Democratic managers

4. Laissez-faire managers

↗ Authoritarian management
+

− Can demotivate staff

A mix of management ....

Fringe Benefits

FRINGE BENEFIT —

Workers have
⬇
They feel
⬇
They are more

Might include:
- staff
- use of
-
-
-

These cost

Section 4 — Human Resources

Mixed Practice Quizzes

It's time to muster up the motivation to tackle some quizzes that cover p.85-92.
Mark each quiz yourself and find out if you need some more training...

Quiz 1 — Date: ...... / ...... / ......

1) What is a person specification?
2) Give one advantage of on-the-job training.
3) What does a paternalistic manager do?
4) Explain how training may increase a worker's motivation.
5) True or false? Using time rate wages encourages staff to work quickly.
6) What does a CV include?
7) Give two benefits of recruiting employees that are well-suited to the role.
8) What is meant by a 'democratic' management style?
9) List three reasons why training staff makes them better at their jobs.
10) What financial incentive gives employees a percentage of a firm's profit?

Total:

Quiz 2 — Date: ...... / ...... / ......

1) Give three things that are included in a job description.
2) Outline what is meant by 'off-the-job training'.
3) How can motivated staff lead to less time and money spent on recruitment and training?
4) What is the purpose of an interview during the selection process?
5) Which management style allows workers to perform tasks as they see fit, offering help as needed?
6) True or false? Good recruitment finds employees with the best skills who will produce high quality output.
7) Give an example of a fringe benefit.
8) Explain how motivating staff can increase productivity.
9) List three things usually included in induction training.
10) Give three advantages of using internal recruitment.

Total:

Mixed Practice Quizzes

Quiz 3 Date: ...... / ...... / ......

1) What term is described as 'any reward for a worker that is not part of their regular income'?
2) Give two disadvantages of using internal recruitment.
3) List three advantages of induction training.
4) Give two benefits of employees taking on greater responsibility after learning new skills.
5) Who shows employees how to do their job during on-the-job training?
6) What does it mean if a worker is paid piece rate wages?
7) Give three benefits to a firm of staff training.
8) What is a salary?
9) Give one disadvantage of an authoritarian management style.
10) What is external recruitment?

Total:

Quiz 4 Date: ...... / ...... / ......

1) Explain why giving workers input into decisions leads to more motivation.
2) What is job analysis?
3) Give one advantage of paying workers a salary.
4) Which type of management style is effective at handling crises?
5) True or false? Off-the-job training is most suitable for learning skills not related to a specific task.
6) What is the term for money paid to sales staff for every item they sell?
7) Give one advantage and one disadvantage of using external recruitment.
8) Outline how on-the-job training works.
9) Give one advantage of paying a worker time rate wages.
10) Outline four steps in the selection process to recruit a new employee.

Total:

Section 5 — Marketing

The Marketing Mix

First Go: ...../...../.....

Four Elements to Marketing

1) Product

The product must fulfil .... or ....

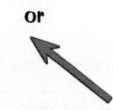

2) ....

Customer must think the product is .... for ....

These four Ps make up the ....

3) ....

Potential customers need to know the product .... and want to .... it.

4) Place

Customers need to be able to .... the product — e.g. in a .... , ... or straight from the ....

Different Marketing Mixes

The .... of the marketing mix affect ....

Some Ps are more .... in .... than others.

.... may pay a higher price if:
- they really .... a ....
- it's in a .... place

.... may pay a lower price if:
- they don't .... a ....
- it's not in a .... place

Adapting Over Time

.... change over time. Businesses should .... their mix to match ....

Many products have .... over time from being .... to being ....

The .... where the .... are bought has also changed (e.g. from .... to ....).

The Marketing Mix

Second Go:
...../...../......

Four Elements to Marketing

①

②
Customer must think

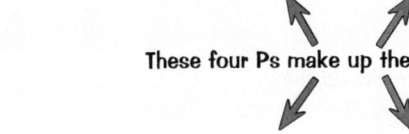

These four Ps make up the

③
Potential customers need to

④
Customers need to be able to

— e.g.

Different Marketing Mixes

The different elements

Some Ps are

Customers may pay a higher price if:
•
•

Customers may pay a lower price if:
•
•

Adapting Over Time

Customers' needs

Many products

The place where the

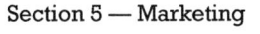

Section 5 — Marketing

Market Research

First Go: ...../...../.....

Structure of Markets

Businesses want to know the _____ of a market.

1. **MARKET** _____ — the _____ of total sales in the market controlled by a business.

2. **MARKET SIZE** — how many potential _____ or _____ of products there are, OR the total _____ of products in a market.

Market Segmentation

SEGMENTATION — when people within a _____ are divided into different _____.

Segmenting a _____ can help a business aim its marketing strategy at its...

_____ **MARKET** — the specific _____ of _____ that a product is aimed at.

Four Ways to Segment a Market

1. Age — customers of different ages have different _____.

2. Income — how much people _____ affects what they will _____.

3. _____ — people who live in different _____ want different products.

4. Gender — _____ can be _____ towards, e.g. women or men.

Using Market Research

Market research helps firms _____ its customers and _____.

- It helps to create a good _____.

- It identifies customers' _____ — products are made that they want to _____.

Market research can stop companies from making _____ (e.g. making too much of a product).

Three benefits of identifying these needs:

1. Increase sales — businesses can _____ pricing based on _____.

2. Stay _____ — gathering information shows _____ between _____, which can improve strategy.

3. Create _____ marketing — businesses can produce more effective _____ material and make relevant _____ for target market.

Section 5 — Marketing

Second Go: ..... / ..... / .....

Market Research

Structure of Markets

Businesses want to know the structure of a market.

1 MARKET SHARE —

2 MARKET SIZE — how many potential

OR

Market Segmentation

SEGMENTATION —

Four Ways to Segment a Market

1 Age —

Segmenting a market can

2 Income —

at its...

TARGET MARKET —

3 Location — people who

Using Market Research

4 Gender —

Market research helps

Three benefits of identifying these   :

- It helps to create

1 .... sales — businesses can

- It identifies customers' .... —

2 Stay .... — gathering information

Market research can .... (e.g. ....).

3 Create targeted marketing —

Section 5 — Marketing

More on Market Research

First Go: ..... / ..... / .....

Market Opportunities

- A market opportunity is where _____ have a need that isn't being _____.
- There are four ways to meet customers' needs before _____:

  1 _____ a new product.

  2 Sell an _____ product in a new _____.

  3 Sell an _____ product at a new _____.

  4 _____ the product differently.

Primary Market Research

PRIMARY RESEARCH — market research that involves getting information from _____ or _____ customers.

↳ E.g. surveys, _____, focus groups, interviews.

+ Advantages
- _____
- relevant and _____ to a product
- can be targeted at specific _____

− Disadvantages
- needs _____ samples to be reliable
- often _____
- _____

Secondary Market Research

SECONDARY RESEARCH — market research that involves looking at data collected by _____.

↳ E.g. market reports, government reports, _____, internet research.

+ Advantages
- _____ than primary research
- easily _____
- instantly available

− Disadvantages
- often _____ of _____
- not always _____
- not _____ to firm's product

Types of Data

QUANTITATIVE DATA — information that can be _____ or reduced to a _____.

QUALITATIVE DATA — information that involves people's _____ or _____. It is hard to _____ opinions, but they give a greater depth of _____.

> Good market research will contain _____ of data.

Section 5 — Marketing

Second Go: ..../..../....

More on Market Research

Market Opportunities

- A market opportunity is where

- There are four ways to meet customers' needs before competitors:

①   ③

②   ④

Primary Market Research

PRIMARY RESEARCH — market research that involves

E.g.

+
-
- relevant and
- can be targeted at

−
- needs large samples to be
-
-

Secondary Market Research

SECONDARY RESEARCH — market research that involves

E.g.

+
- cheaper than
-
-

−
- often
-
-

Types of Data

QUANTITATIVE DATA — information that

QUALITATIVE DATA — information that

It is hard to compare opinions, but they

> Good market research will
> ....

Section 5 — Marketing

Product Life Cycles

First Go: ...../...../.....

Five Stages of Product Life Cycles

PRODUCT LIFE CYCLE — the different _____ that a product goes through over _____.

1 _____ (R&D) — idea is _____ and turned into a product. One aim is to find the most _____ way to make the product.

During R&D, big firms _____ people who try to use _____ discoveries to develop new products.

2 Introduction — product goes on _____. A lot of focus on _____ to increase _____.

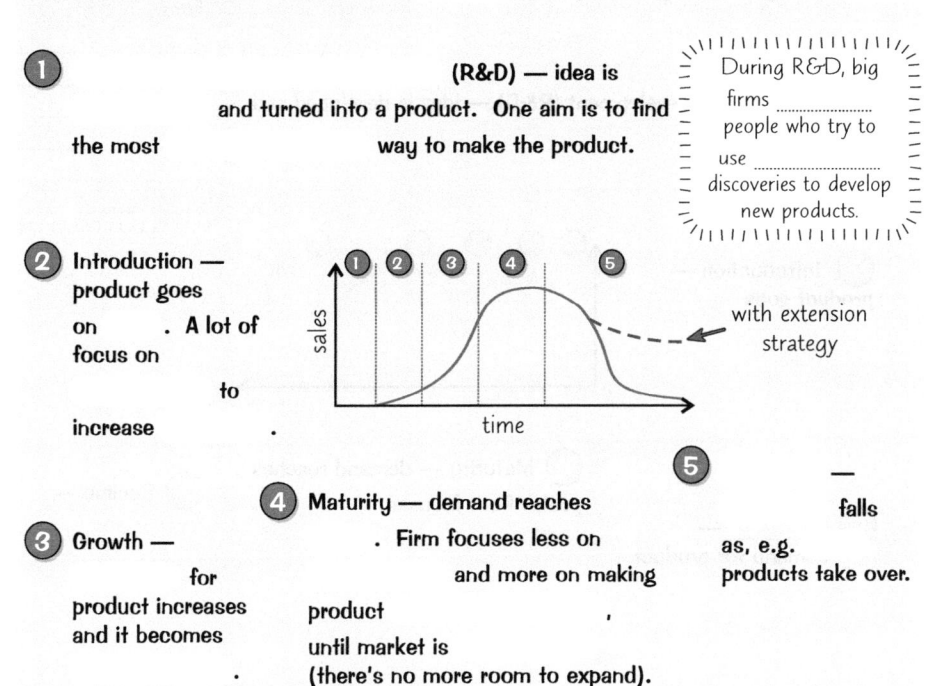

_____ with extension strategy

3 Growth — _____ for product increases and it becomes _____.

4 Maturity — demand reaches _____. Firm focuses less on _____ and more on making product _____, until market is _____ (there's no more room to expand).

5 _____ — _____ falls as, e.g. _____ products take over.

Profit and Loss During the Product Life Cycle

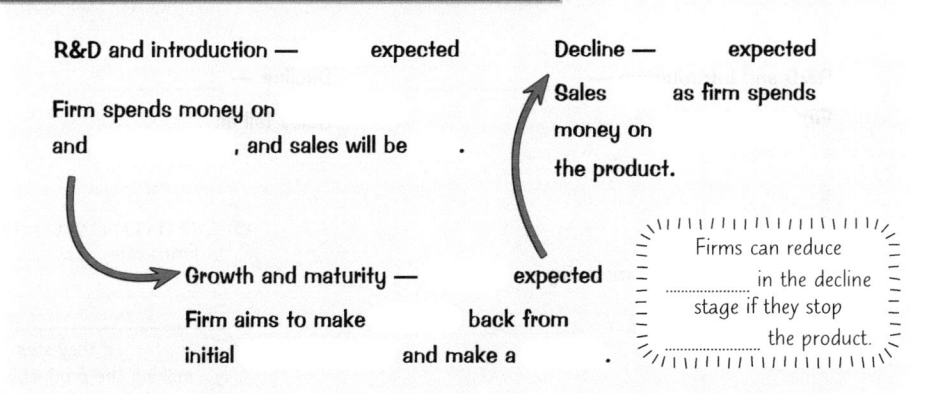

R&D and introduction — _____ expected
Firm spends money on _____ and _____, and sales will be _____.

Growth and maturity — _____ expected
Firm aims to make back from initial _____ and make a _____.

Decline — _____ expected
Sales _____ as firm spends money on _____ the product.

Firms can reduce _____ in the decline stage if they stop _____ the product.

Section 5 — Marketing

102

Second Go:
..... / ..... / .....

Product Life Cycles

Five Stages of Product Life Cycles

PRODUCT LIFE CYCLE —

During R&D, big firms ....

1) **Research and Development (R&D)** — idea is developed and

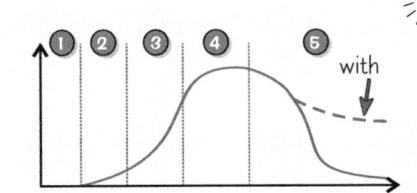

2) **Introduction** — product goes

3) .... — demand for product

4) **Maturity** — demand reaches peak. Firm focuses

5) **Decline** —

Profit and Loss During the Product Life Cycle

R&D and introduction — ....
Firm spends

Growth and maturity — ....
Firm aims to

Decline — ....
Sales fall as

Firms can .... if they stop making the product.

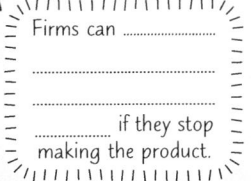

Section 5 — Marketing

Extension Strategies

First Go: ..... / ..... / .....

Extending the Life of a Product

EXTENSION STRATEGY — when a firm takes action to .... the .... of a .... product.

If extension strategy works, product keeps .... and makes a .... for longer.

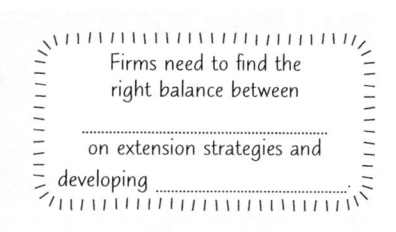

> Firms need to find the right balance between .... on extension strategies and developing ....

Five Types of Extension Strategy

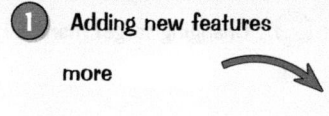

1 Adding new features

more ....

↘ increase in ....

more .... ↗

2 Using .... packaging

more ....

↓

more likely to see it

3 Changing ....

e.g. promote in a different .... or country

4 Changing advertising

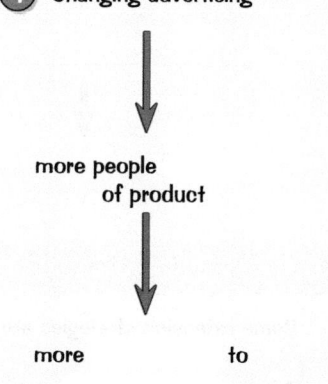

more people .... of product

↓

more .... to ....

5 Lowering ....

e.g. reducing .... , or running special .... and competitions

Combining Extension Strategies

Some extension strategies are .... to one another.

E.g. changing .... or .... will help to .... target a ....

Businesses must evaluate the .... of strategies that will .... the .... of their products.

Section 5 — Marketing

Second Go:
..... / ..... / .....

Extension Strategies

Extending the Life of a Product

EXTENSION STRATEGY —

If extension strategy works,

Firms need to find .... on extension strategies and ....

Five Types of Extension Strategy

1) Adding ....

   .... increase in ....

2) Using ....

   ↓

   customers ....

3) Changing target market
   e.g.

4) Changing advertising

   ↓

   more people ....
   ....

   ↓

   more ....
   ....

5) .... prices
   e.g.

Combining Extension Strategies

Some extension strategies are

↘ E.g.

Businesses must evaluate the

Section 5 — Marketing

Mixed Practice Quizzes

Give these quiz questions a go to test your knowledge of p.95-104. Mark each quiz yourself to see what stage of the business revision life cycle you're on.

Quiz 1 — Date: ...... / ...... / ......

1) Give two reasons why adding new features to a product leads to an increase in demand.
2) What is primary market research?
3) What are the four Ps in the marketing mix?
4) Why might a firm segment a market by income?
5) Which stages of the product life cycle is profit expected in?
6) True or false? Firms must evaluate what combination of extension strategies best suit their products.
7) What is meant by 'market share'?
8) What is an extension strategy?
9) Give three advantages of using secondary market research.
10) How can firms reduce losses in the decline stage of the product life cycle?

Total:

Quiz 2 — Date: ...... / ...... / ......

1) State the five stages of a product's life cycle.
2) What happens if an extension strategy for a product is successful?
3) Give an example of a question that gives quantitative data.
4) What are three benefits of using market research to identify customers' needs?
5) In which stage of the product life cycle does demand reach its peak?
6) Surveys and questionnaires are examples of what type of market research?
7) List five examples of extension strategies.
8) True or false? The four elements of the marketing mix are: product, price, promotion and people.
9) What is qualitative data?
10) Why is price important for attracting customers?

Total:

Section 5 — Marketing

Mixed Practice Quizzes

Quiz 3   Date: ...... / ...... / ......

1) What is quantitative data?
2) Give three disadvantages of using primary market research.
3) How does market research help keep a firm competitive?
4) What stage of the product life cycle comes after growth?
5) How does changing advertising extend the life of a product?
6) List four ways to segment a market.
7) What is the importance of promotion for the marketing mix?
8) True or false? Firms need to balance spending on extension strategies and spending on developing new products.
9) In what part of a product's life cycle does demand for the product fall?
10) What is market segmentation?

Total:

Quiz 4   Date: ...... / ...... / ......

1) What happens during the introduction stage of a product's life cycle?
2) What is meant by a 'target market'?
3) Suggest how the place a product is sold can affect the price customers pay.
4) What is meant by a 'product life cycle'?
5) Give an example of how one extension strategy can affect another.
6) Give three disadvantages of using secondary market research.
7) Outline how businesses adapt their marketing mix to match customers' needs over time.
8) Why might a firm use new packaging as part of an extension strategy?
9) True or false? Big firms hire scientists during the R&D stage of the product life cycle.
10) Give four ways a market opportunity can be met.

Total:

Product Portfolios

First Go: ..... / ..... / .....

Range of Products

PRODUCT PORTFOLIO — _____ of different products a business _____ .

Businesses want a _____ product portfolio. This includes:

1. a _____ of different products

2. products at _____ stages of the _____

So if one product _____ , they can still _____ on others.

Four Product Types in a Boston Matrix

BOSTON MATRIX (or BOSTON BOX) — a way to _____ a business's product portfolio.

1. Question marks — _____ market share and _____ market growth. New products, so aren't _____ yet and need heavy _____ to succeed.

2. _____ — low market share and growth. Mainly lost _____ .

3. Cash cows — _____ market share and _____ market growth. Very _____ , _____ are low and are produced in high _____ .

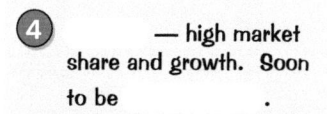

4. _____ — high market share and growth. Soon to be _____ .

Each circle represents one product. The size shows the revenue.

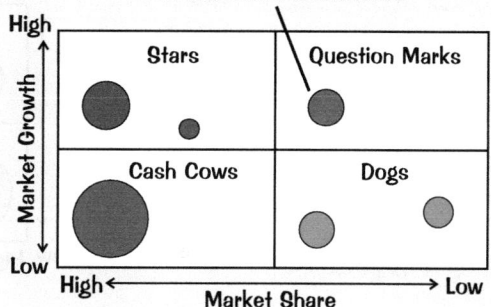

(Boston Matrix diagram with Market Growth on vertical axis (Low to High) and Market Share on horizontal axis (High to Low), showing four quadrants: Stars, Question Marks, Cash Cows, Dogs)

Using a Boston Matrix

+ Helps to see whether a _____ has a _____ product portfolio.

+ Identifies how to _____ a portfolio, e.g. _____ stars or cash cows.

− Can be _____ , e.g. a dog can still be _____ despite low market share.

Section 5 — Marketing

| Second Go: ..../..../.... |

Product Portfolios

Range of Products

PRODUCT PORTFOLIO — range

Businesses want a balanced product portfolio. This includes:

①

②

So if one product

Four Product Types in a Boston Matrix

BOSTON MATRIX (or BOSTON BOX) —

Each circle represents one product. The size shows the revenue.

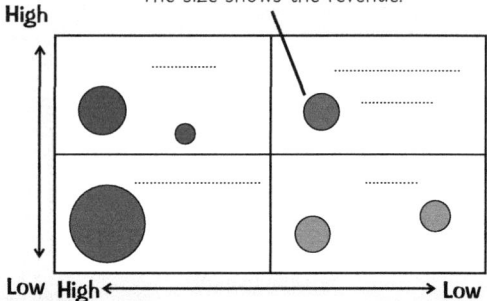

① Question marks —

② Dogs —

③ Cash cows —

④ Stars —

Using a Boston Matrix

➕ Helps to see

➕ Identifies

➖

Section 5 — Marketing

Product Development

First Go: ..... / ..... / .....

Developing New Products

- High _____ products eventually begin to _____
- So businesses should have products in _____ and _____ stages.
- These grow to _____ and take place of the _____ products.

_____ firms make new products from market research.
_____ firms invent new things and try to sell them.

Benefits and Risks of Developing New Products

+
- Increase in _____.
- May _____ to new market.
- _____ prices charged if product is brought to market before _____.
- _____ gain if a firm always releases products before its _____.

−
- _____ and _____ if too much time spent in R&D.
- Can waste _____ making something customers don't want.
- Product may not be able to be made at a _____ scale at a low enough _____.
- _____ loss if new product is _____ quality.

Brand Image

- Strong brand images are easily _____ and liked by _____.
- The _____ must be right to have a _____ brand image.
- Gives a reputation for high _____, keeping customers _____.

Firms spend _____ and lots of money building a _____ brand image.

Product Differentiation

- If a product isn't _____, customers think it is _____ to others.
- They have no _____ to buy the product, unless it's _____.

UNIQUE SELLING POINT (USP) — a _____ that makes the product _____ from competitors'.

Three factors of the _____ help with product differentiation.

1 _____ — design is fit for purpose, can contain _____ features.

2 Cost — good _____ will lead to _____ manufacturing costs.

3 Appearance — _____ can help a product stand out.

Section 5 — Marketing

Second Go: ..... / ..... / .....

Product Development

Developing New Products

- High selling products

- So businesses should have

- These grow to

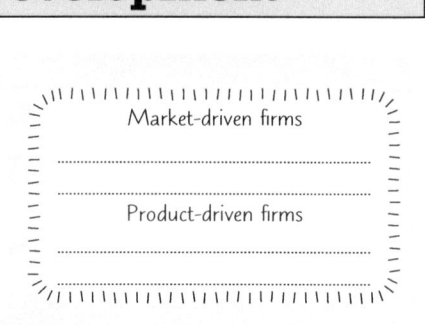

> Market-driven firms
>
> ....
>
> Product-driven firms
>
> ....

Benefits and Risks of Developing New Products

+
-
-
- Higher prices charged if

- Reputation gain if

−
- Costly and time consuming if

-

- Product may not be able to be made at

- Reputation loss if

Brand Image

- Strong brand images are

- The marketing mix must be right to

- Gives a reputation for

> Firms spend many years and
> ....
> ....

① Function —   ② Cost —

Product Differentiation

- If a product isn't distinct,

- They have no reason

UNIQUE SELLING POINT (USP)
—

Three factors of the design mix help with product differentiation.

③ Appearance —

Section 5 — Marketing

Price

First Go:
...../...../.....

Price and Demand

DEMAND (for a product) — how .... customers are .... of the product ....

As the .... of a product rises, ... for it tends to fall.

Firms risk not .... many products if their prices are ....

Internal Factors Affecting Prices

1) **Aims and ....**
   If a business wants to:
   - increase .... , it may .... its prices.
   - expand, it might set prices .... to .... to fund ....

2) **Internal ....**
   - E.g. buying .... can .... costs in the long term.
   - Prices can then be .... , but still ....

3) **Product ....**
   E.g. if the product is in the decline stage, the price may be .... to .... again.

4) **Changes to ....**
   E.g. when .... a .... product, prices may be .... for a period.

External Factors Affecting Prices

1) **Nature of the ....**
   E.g. a .... can fetch a .... than a similar, ...

2) **Competition**
   - Prices can't be much higher than .... prices.
   - They also can't be much lower — customers will ....

3) **............ costs**
   E.g. if costs of .... increase, prices may need to .... to make a profit.

The .... and .... of the business also affect pricing. E.g. a larger, ... firm might have .... customers who are willing to pay slightly .... They can also benefit from .... to help keep .... down.

Section 5 — Marketing

Price

Second Go:
..... /..... /.....

Price and Demand

DEMAND (for a product) —

As the

→ Firms risk

Internal Factors Affecting Prices

1. **Aims and objectives**
   If a business wants to:
   •
   •

2. **Internal costs**
   •
   •

3. **Product life cycle**
   E.g. if the product is in

4. **Changes to marketing mix**
   E.g. when promoting a

External Factors Affecting Prices

1. **Nature of the market**

2. **Competition**
   •
   •

3. **External costs**

> The size and .... E.g. a larger, older firm ....
> .... They can also ....
> ....
> ....

Section 5 — Marketing

Pricing Strategies

First Go: ..... / ..... / .....

Price Penetration

Firm charges .... price when product is ....

⬇

Helps increase .... and establish ....

⬇

Once product is established, firm .... price to make ....

Price Skimming

Firm charges .... price when product is new as they know the .... will be high, e.g. because the firm has .... customers or the product uses .... , sought-after ....

↘

.... price helps increase .... and cover .... cost of ....

↘

Firm .... price once product is .... to reach a .... market.

Loss Leader Pricing

Price of product is set .... the cost of .... it, so firm makes a .... on each sale.
Firm assumes that selling the product will increase .... of other, ... products.

> E.g. new games consoles are often sold at a ...., but the firm makes a .... on .... bought for them.

Competitive Pricing

Firm charges .... price to other firms.
Usually happens if the market is very .... and there isn't much ....

Usually means .... is made.
Firm has to find ways other than .... to .... customers, e.g. by providing ....

> A .... price might also make the product more .... to people with .... — this can improve the firm's .... and ....

Cost-Plus Pricing

Firm decides price based on how much .... they want (while keeping .... high enough). Often happens when firm faces little ....

They could decide price by:

1 Using a .... — adding .... on a certain .... to the cost of making the product.

2 Deciding on their desired .... and calculating the .... required for it.

Section 5 — Marketing

Pricing Strategies

Second Go: ...../...../.....

Price Penetration

⬇

⬇

Once product is established,

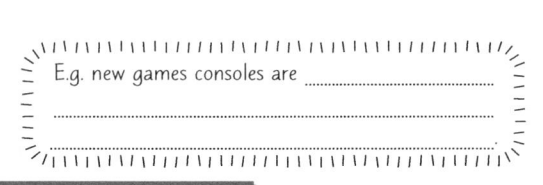

Price Skimming

Firm charges high price when

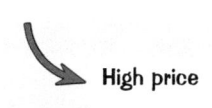

➘ High price

Loss Leader Pricing

Price of product is set

Firm assumes that

> E.g. new games consoles are ....
> ....
> ....

Competitive Pricing

Firm charges similar price to other firms. Usually happens if

Usually means little profit is made. Firm has to

> A .... price might also make the product more desirable to .... — this can improve the ....

➘

Cost-Plus Pricing

Firm decides price based on how much

They could decide price by:

① Using a mark-up —

② Deciding on their

Section 5 — Marketing

Mixed Practice Quizzes

A fresh bunch of questions for you to try covering p.107-114 here. Mark each quiz yourself, then you can see how balanced your knowledge portfolio is...

Quiz 1 — Date: ...... / ...... / ......

1) Give two benefits to a firm of developing new products.
2) List five types of pricing strategy.
3) What is the relationship between the price of a product and demand for it?
4) State the four product types in a Boston Matrix.
5) Why should businesses always have products in the development and introduction stages?
6) Which pricing strategy involves charging a low price when a product is new, and increasing the price when it is established?
7) Give two features of a balanced product portfolio.
8) What type of product has high market share and low market growth?
9) True or false? Firms never charge less for a product than it costs to make it.
10) Give an example of how the internal costs of a firm affect prices.

Total:

Quiz 2 — Date: ...... / ...... / ......

1) What is meant by the 'demand' for a product?
2) Outline how a loss leader pricing strategy works.
3) What is a product portfolio?
4) Describe the cost aspect of the design mix.
5) True or false? High prices can make a product more desirable to customers with higher incomes.
6) Give three external factors that can affect the price of a product.
7) How can firms get 'question mark' products to succeed?
8) Which pricing strategy involves charging a high price for a new product, then reducing the price once it is established?
9) State four potential risks to a firm when developing new products.
10) Explain the benefit to a firm of having a strong brand image.

Total:

Section 5 — Marketing

Mixed Practice Quizzes

Quiz 3 Date: …… / …… / ……

1) Explain how the cost of raw materials can affect the price of a product.
2) What type of product has low market share and a high market growth?
3) Give one example of a product that might be sold using a loss leader pricing strategy.
4) State four internal factors that may affect the price of a product.
5) Explain two ways a firm can set its prices using cost-plus pricing.
6) State the three factors of the design mix.
7) Outline how a competitive pricing strategy works.
8) Explain why product differentiation is important.
9) True or false? A dog is usually more profitable than a cash cow.
10) Give one reason why a larger, older firm may be able to charge higher prices.

Total:

Quiz 4 Date: …… / …… / ……

1) What market conditions allow a firm to use a cost-plus pricing strategy?
2) True or false? A luxury product can fetch a higher price than a similar, non-luxury product.
3) Describe the function aspect of the design mix.
4) Explain why a firm might charge a high price for a new product as part of a price skimming strategy.
5) What does the size of a circle on a Boston Matrix represent?
6) What is a unique selling point?
7) Outline how a price penetration pricing strategy works.
8) Why can a Boston Matrix be misleading?
9) How are market-driven firms different to product-driven firms?
10) Outline how competition may affect the price of a product.

Total:

Section 5 — Marketing

Methods of Promotion

First Go: ...../...../.....

Four Reasons for Promoting a Product

1. To inform — so customers know the product _____, its _____ and _____.
2. To persuade — firms tempt customers to _____ their product over a _____. Tactics can include displaying _____ and _____.
3. To create or change the _____ — depending on who the product is _____.
4. To create or increase sales — _____ sales leads to more _____ and _____.

Six Methods of Advertising

ADVERTISING — any message that a firm _____ for to _____ itself or its products.

1. **Newspapers**
   Reach wide audience (_____) or specific market (_____), but poor print _____ and _____ reader numbers.

2. **Magazines**
   _____ than newspaper adverts, but better _____ and targeted at specific _____.

3. **Posters/**_____
   Can be placed near a _____ audience and get seen _____, but messages need to be _____.

4. _____/flyers/business cards
   _____ to produce and can be targeted at specific _____, but many people see them as _____.

5. _____
   Can deliver _____ message to wide audience, but very _____.

6. **Internet**
   Can reach _____ and _____ audiences, and customers can click straight through to firm's _____. But many people ignore or _____ them.

Sponsorship

SPONSORSHIP — when a firm gives _____ to an _____ or _____ in return for their name being _____.

+ _____ can help raise firm's _____

− _____ can suffer if thing being sponsored gets _____

Section 5 — Marketing

Second Go: ..../..../....

Methods of Promotion

Four Reasons for Promoting a Product

1. To inform —

2. To persuade —

3. To create or change the .... —

4. To create or increase .... —

Six Methods of Advertising

ADVERTISING — ....
....

1. Newspapers

2. Magazines

3. Posters/billboards

4. Leaflets/flyers/business cards

5. Television

6. Internet

Sponsorship

SPONSORSHIP — when a firm

+ can help

— brand image

Section 5 — Marketing

More Methods of Promotion

First Go: ...../...../.....

Six Methods of Promotion

1. Competitions
2. .... offers
3. Free ....
4. Coupons
5. .... displays
6. Free ....

Public Relations (PR)

PUBLIC RELATIONS — activities that involve .... with the .... to promote a firm or its .... to the ....

+ PR is a .... , easy way for a firm to get .... by a wide ....
− There's .... control over how the media .... — e.g. interviews can be ....

+ • encourages customers to try product
  • .... in short term
  • can .... in long term if .... customers become ....

− • customers might not want to .... product when it's at ....
  • might not be .... for certain .... (it makes it feel less of a ....)

Social Media

Firms use social media to .... products, offer .... or .... to build excitement on .... products.

+ • Can add .... at any time.
  • Customers can .... to a firm's website to ....

− .... can be seen by .... of people, so firms must .... sites.

• .... market — promotions need to be .... and appeal to the right ....
• .... of the market — firms may spend .... on growing markets.

Promotional Mix

PROMOTIONAL MIX — the combination of .... methods used to .... a product.

Factors that affect .... promotional mix:

• .... available — large firms usually have .... money to spend.
• .... of the product — some products need .... descriptions.
• Competition — firms may .... what their .... are doing.

Section 5 — Marketing

Second Go: ..../..../....

More Methods of Promotion

Six Methods of Promotion

1.
2.
3.
4.
5.
6.

+ • encourages new

• boosts sales in

•

Public Relations (PR)

PUBLIC RELATIONS —

+ PR is

− There's little

− •

• might not be suitable

Social Media

Firms use social media to

+ • Can add
• Customers

− Negative

• Target market —

• Nature of the market —

Promotional Mix

PROMOTIONAL MIX —

Factors that affect promotional mix:
• Finance available —

• Nature of the product —

• Competition — firms may

Section 5 — Marketing

Place

First Go: ..../..../.....

Channels of Distribution

CHANNEL OF DISTRIBUTION — the way
get from a .... to a ....

Firms choose a channel based on:
- consumers .... are likely ....
- how much .... is needed
- they want to .... to consumers
- consumers they want to reach

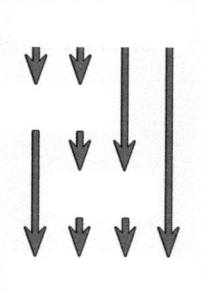

Wholesalers

Manufacturers who make .... of a product often .... to wholesalers.

➕ **Advantages**
- manufacturers don't need to .... lots of ....
- wholesalers have .... customers, so products .... customers
- retailers .... from wholesalers, reaching .... customers

➖ **Disadvantage**
consumers may get .... levels of ....

Retailers

Manufacturers who .... to retailers can provide them with product ....

➕ **Advantages**
- good .... , so high .... with products
- retailers can .... products to .... sales
- products are sold in many .... , exposing them to lots of .... customers

➖ **Disadvantage**
hard for .... manufacturers to get retailers to .... their products

Telesales

Manufacturers who make .... items or have .... customers may use telesales — they sell products .... to consumers via ....

➕ **Advantage**
consumers may get a better .... than buying from a .... or ....

➖ **Disadvantages**
- .... to sell to individuals
- .... to arrange .... of goods

Section 5 — Marketing

Second Go: ..../..../.....

Place

Channels of Distribution

CHANNEL OF DISTRIBUTION —

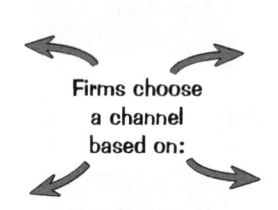

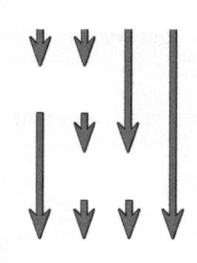

Firms choose a channel based on:

Wholesalers

Manufacturers who make

+ • manufacturers

• wholesalers

• retailers

— consumers may get

Retailers

Manufacturers who sell to

+ • good

• retailers can

• products are sold in

— hard for consumers

Telesales

Manufacturers who make

+ •

— •

Section 5 — Marketing

E-Commerce

First Go: ..... / ..... / .....

Buying Online

Customers can .... to buy online.
- Firms list .... on a .... or ....
- Customers .... or follow a .... directly to a ....
- Products are .... and .... for, e.g. using a ....
- Products are .... to the customer.

.... allow customers to shop online .... they are.

Customers expect:
- to be able to .... from a firm
- low ....
- free .... and ....
- an .... website

Growth of E-Commerce

E-commerce and m-commerce (............ commerce) are ....

More consumers have access to the .... and it is becoming more ....

↓

.... consumers are buying products ....

↓

Businesses must .... to keep up with changing .... and ....

Customers are able to:
- buy from firms ....
- easily .... products and .... on different ....

Customers will .... if a firm doesn't meet their .... or a .... can .... them.

Reasons for Using E-Commerce

➕ Advantages

- easy access to .... markets — more potential .... , so .... may increase
- saves money on ....
- reduced .... and .... costs if high street shops ....
- can relocate offices to areas with ....
- savings mean .... can be offered than a high street shop

➖ Disadvantages

- .... needs to be bought and ....
- specialist website or app need to be ....
- staff need .... in using .... to provide good ....
- some consumers are .... to buy online and prefer ....

Section 5 — Marketing

Second Go:
...../...../.....

E-Commerce

Buying Online

Customers can choose ....

- Firms

- Customers

- Products

- Products

> Smartphones ....
> ....

Customers expect:
-
-
-
-

Growth of E-Commerce

E-commerce and

More

More

Customers are able to:
-
-

> Customers will ....
> ....
> or ....

Reasons for Using E-Commerce

+ easy access to

-

- reduced

- can relocate

- savings mean

-

-

-

-

Section 5 — Marketing

Mixed Practice Quizzes

It's time to channel the distribution of knowledge straight from your brain to these quizzes that test p.117-124. Mark each quiz yourself and find your total score.

Quiz 1 — Date: ...... / ...... / ......

1) What is meant by 'public relations'?
2) True or false? More consumers having access to the internet has lead to a growth in e-commerce and m-commerce.
3) Name two tactics a firm can use to persuade customers to choose their products over competitors.
4) Give two disadvantages to firms using telesales.
5) List six different methods of advertising a firm could use.
6) What is the promotional mix?
7) Give one disadvantage of using retailers as a channel of distribution.
8) Give two advantages of a firm using social media to advertise products.
9) How can using e-commerce allow firms to offer lower prices than high street shops?
10) Give one advantage and one disadvantage of using posters to advertise.

Total:

Quiz 2 — Date: ...... / ...... / ......

1) Give one advantage for a manufacturer using a wholesaler.
2) List four reasons why a firm would promote a product.
3) What is advertising?
4) Give one advantage to a firm using public relations.
5) List four expectations that customers have when buying online.
6) What is meant by 'sponsorship'?
7) True or false? Manufacturers who make lots of a product often sell straight to retailers.
8) Why must firms monitor their social media?
9) Give one advantage and one disadvantage of using television to advertise.
10) How does the nature of the market affect a firm's promotional mix?

Total:

Section 5 — Marketing

Mixed Practice Quizzes

Quiz 3 Date: ...... / ...... / ......

1) List five advantages to firms of using e-commerce.
2) What term describes a firm giving money to an organisation or event in exchange for the firm's name being displayed.
3) How does the nature of a product affect a firm's promotional mix?
4) Give one disadvantage of using wholesalers as a channel of distribution.
5) List six methods of promotion.
6) What is a 'channel of distribution'?
7) Give one advantage to a firm using sponsorship to promote its products.
8) True or false? Customers expect low prices and an easy-to-use website when purchasing products online.
9) Give one disadvantage of public relations.
10) Outline why a firm might advertise in a magazine over a newspaper.

Total:

Quiz 4 Date: ...... / ...... / ......

1) Why might firms avoid some methods of promotion for luxury items?
2) Give one disadvantage to a firm using sponsorship for promotion.
3) List four disadvantages to firms using e-commerce.
4) Give two advantages of manufacturers channelling their distribution through retailers.
5) Outline the steps a customer takes to buy products from a firm's website.
6) True or false? PR is an easy way for a firm to get noticed by a wide audience, but it is usually very expensive.
7) Give one advantage and one disadvantage of using the internet to advertise.
8) Give four things a firm considers when choosing a channel of distribution.
9) List five factors that affect the promotional mix.
10) Why would a consumer buy a product through telesales instead of through wholesalers or retailers?

Total:

Section 5 — Marketing

Section 6 — Finance

Sources of Finance

First Go: ...../...../.....

Five Reasons New or Small Businesses Need Finance

1. Start-up _____ to set up the business.
2. To cover poor initial _____
3. To cover a _____ in cash, e.g. because of _____ payments from customers.
4. To cover day-to-day costs of struggling businesses.
5. To _____ the business, e.g. to pay for new _____ or _____.

Government Grants

- Grants are typically given to _____ or _____ firms.
- They do not have to be _____.
- _____ criteria needed for firms to qualify.
- May have to _____ money in a _____ way.

Long-Term Sources

Three types of loans:

1. **Bank loans**
   + _____ and _____, lower _____ than overdrafts.
   − Bank can repossess _____ if not repaid.

2. **Friends and family**
   + Money goes into firm _____.
   − Lender may expect a _____ in profits.

3. **Mortgages** — used to finance _____.
   + Interest is _____.
   − Property used as _____.

Short-Term Sources

_____ credit — paying suppliers one or two months _____ the purchase.
+ time to earn money to _____ debt
− late repayment = large _____

Overdrafts — taking _____ money out of a bank account than is actually in it.
+ can make payments _____ without having the cash
− high _____, bank can _____ overdraft, bank can repossess _____ if not paid back

Hire purchase — _____ paid and rest is paid in _____ over time.
- Firm has _____ use of a product.
- Can use a product they couldn't otherwise _____.

Long-term sources are good for a firm's _____

Sources of Finance

Second Go: ..... / ..... / .....

Five Reasons New or Small Businesses Need Finance

1. Start-up capital
2. To cover poor
3. To cover a
4. To cover day-to-day
5.

Government Grants

- Grants are
- They do not
-
- May have to

Long-Term Sources

Three types of loans:

1. Bank loans
   + Quick and
   − Bank can

2. Friends and family
   +
   − Lender may

3. Mortgages —
   +
   −

Short-Term Sources

Trade credit —
+
−

Overdrafts —
+
−

Hire purchase —
- Firm has
-

Long-term sources are ....

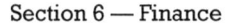

Section 6 — Finance

More Sources of Finance

First Go: ...../...../.....

Three Sources for Established Firms

① RETAINED .... — .... that are .... into the firm.
- Owners .... profits after ....
- .... companies give large .... to shareholders.

> Established firms are .... to go bankrupt, so are less risky for banks to .... to.

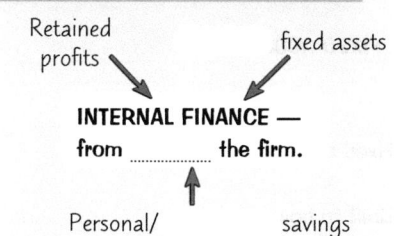

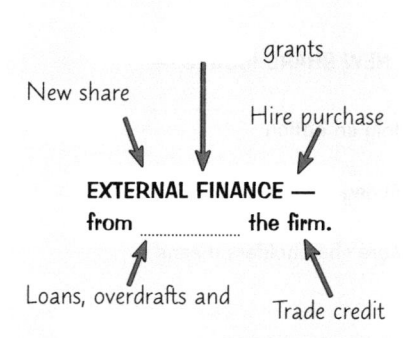

② .... ASSETS — assets that a business keeps ...., e.g. machinery or ....
- .... assets that aren't being used can be ....
- .... to how much can be .... — some are needed to keep ....

③ NEW SHARE ISSUES — .... raised through .... new shares.
- Only an option for .... companies.
- Money raised doesn't need to be ....
- More shareholders means less .... for existing ....

Internal and External Finance

Retained profits ↘   fixed assets ↙
INTERNAL FINANCE — .... from .... the firm.
↑
Personal/............... savings

.... grants
New share ....   Hire purchase
EXTERNAL FINANCE — .... from .... the firm.
↑
Loans, overdrafts and ....   Trade credit

Four Factors Affecting Choice

① Size and .... of business
Not all firms can access all types of .... Some firms have no fixed assets or cannot issue ....

② .... of finance
E.g. .... or .... useful to cover for short lengths of time.

③ Amount of money needed
- Small amounts from ....
- Large amounts from ....

④ Cost of the finance
Some sources are more .... than others, e.g. bank loans and ....

Section 6 — Finance

Second Go: ..... / ..... / .....

More Sources of Finance

Three Sources for Established Firms

1) RETAINED PROFITS —
-
-

Internal and External Finance

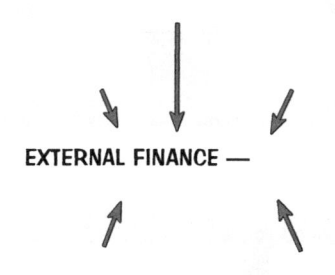

INTERNAL FINANCE —

EXTERNAL FINANCE —

Established firms are ....

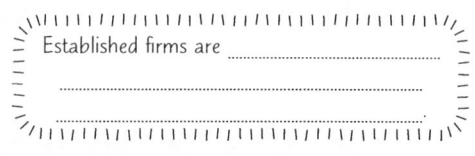

2) FIXED ASSETS —

- Fixed assets that
- Limit to how much

3) NEW SHARE ISSUES —

- Only an option
- Money raised
- More shareholders means

Four Factors Affecting Choice

1) Size and type of business
Not all firms can

2) Duration of finance
E.g.

3) Amount of money needed
- Small
- Large

4) Cost of the finance
Some sources are

e.g.

Section 6 — Finance

Investments

First Go: ...../...../.....

Investment Projects

INVESTMENT — money put into a business to make _____ that make the business more _____.

Three examples are:

1) New machinery
- able to make _____
- _____ more _____ processes

2) New buildings
- increase number of _____
- increase amount of _____
- increase amount of _____ held

3) New vehicles
- _____ vehicles
- _____ vehicles

Average Rate of Return

RETURN ON INVESTMENT — how much a business _____ or _____ as a proportion of the _____ put in.

AVERAGE RATE OF RETURN (ARR) — the _____ investment each _____ on an _____ over its lifespan.

Two steps to calculate ARR:

1) Work out the _____ annual profit.

$$\frac{\text{..................}}{\text{annual profit}} = \frac{\quad\quad\quad\quad}{\quad\quad\quad\quad}$$

2) Use the formula to find ARR.

$$\text{ARR (\%)} = \frac{\quad\quad\quad\quad}{\quad\quad\quad\quad} \times 100$$

EXAMPLE

The table below shows the profit made by a business on a £2m investment over three years. Calculate the average rate of return for the investment.

	Profit (£)
Year 1	70 000
Year 2	95 000
Year 3	105 000

1) average annual profit = $\frac{\quad\quad\quad\quad}{\quad\quad\quad\quad}$ = $\frac{70\,000 + 95\,000 + \quad}{\quad\quad}$

= _____ ÷ _____ = £ _____

2) average rate of return = $\frac{\quad\quad\quad\quad}{\quad\quad\quad\quad} \times 100 = \frac{\quad\quad\quad}{2\,000\,000} \times 100$

= _____ × 100 = _____ %

☹ ☑   😐 ☑   🙂 ☑

Section 6 — Finance

Second Go: ..../..../....

Investments

Investment Projects

INVESTMENT —

Three examples are:

1. New machinery
   - able to
   -

2. New buildings
   - increase
   - increase
   - increase

3. New vehicles
   - more
   -

Average Rate of Return

RETURN ON INVESTMENT —

AVERAGE RATE OF RETURN (ARR) —

Two steps to calculate ARR:

1. Work out the

   =

2. Use the formula to find   .

   =

EXAMPLE

The table below shows the profit made by a business on a £2m investment over three years. Calculate the average rate of return for the investment.

	Profit (£)
Year 1	70 000
Year 2	95 000
Year 3	105 000

1. average annual profit =   =

   =   =

2. average rate of return =

   =   =   =

Section 6 — Finance

Mixed Practice Quizzes

Test the return on your studying by trying out these quizzes covering p.127-132.
Mark each quiz, find your score, and check your net knowledge increase.

Quiz 1   Date: ...... / ...... / ......

1) True or false? A firm can raise money by issuing new shares.
2)* Calculate the average annual profit for a firm that made a total of £1 200 000 profit over four years.
3) Give two ways that new buildings can increase the profitability of a firm.
4) How can fixed assets be used as an internal source of finance?
5) True or false? Long-term sources of finance are good for a firm's cash flow.
6)* A firm invests £1 000 000 and makes an average annual profit of £400 000 on the investment. What is the ARR on this investment?
7) Give one advantage of using bank loans as a source of finance.
8) Why should businesses consider the cost of a source of finance?
9) Give one source of finance that is useful for a short length of time.
10) What type of firms are government grants typically given to?

Total:

Quiz 2   Date: ...... / ...... / ......

1) List four factors that affect a firm's choice of finance.
2)* Calculate the average annual profit for a firm that made a total of £2 400 000 profit over 6 years.
3) List three sources of internal finance.
4) Give one advantage of using an overdraft as a source of finance.
5) Give three reasons why a new business might need to arrange finance.
6) What is meant by the 'average rate of return'?
7) Give one disadvantage of using government grants as a source of finance.
8) What is trade credit?
9) Why might larger businesses be less able to use retained profits as a source of finance?
10) List two ways that new machinery can make a firm more profitable.

Total:

Section 6 — Finance

Mixed Practice Quizzes

Quiz 3 Date: ...... / ...... / ......

1) Give two advantages of using hire purchase.
2) Name three sources of external finance.
3)* Calculate the ARR for an investment if the total profit over 4 years is £2 000 000, and the cost of investment was £5 000 000.
4) What are retained profits?
5) How does issuing new shares affect the control of the owners of a firm?
6) List three types of investment project.
7) What is the expression $\frac{\text{average annual profit}}{\text{cost of investment}} \times 100$ used to calculate?
8) What is meant by the term 'investment'?
9) Give one disadvantage of using a mortgage as a source of finance.
10) Give an example of a situation that might result in a shortfall of cash for a firm.

Total:

Quiz 4 Date: ...... / ...... / ......

1)* A firm makes £900 000 over 3 years. Find the average annual profit.
2) True or false? Government grants are an internal source of finance.
3) What does it mean when a firm uses an overdraft?
4) Give one advantage of a firm issuing new shares as a source of finance.
5) Give three types of loan a firm can take out.
6) What limits the ability of a firm to use fixed assets as a source of finance?
7) What may friends or family expect of a firm if they have loaned some money to it?
8) What is meant by 'return on investment'?
9)* A firm had an average annual profit of £2 000 000 on an investment of £4 000 000. What is the ARR on this investment?
10) What is meant by 'hire purchase'?

Total:

Section 6 — Finance

Break-Even Analysis

First Go: ..../..../....

Break-Even Output

BREAK-EVEN OUTPUT — the level of output a business needs to _____.

- Selling more than break-even output = _____.
- Selling less than break-even output = _____.
- New businesses should do a break-even _____ to find the break-even _____.

> A low break-even output means a business doesn't have to _____ to _____.

Features of Break-Even Chart

EXAMPLE

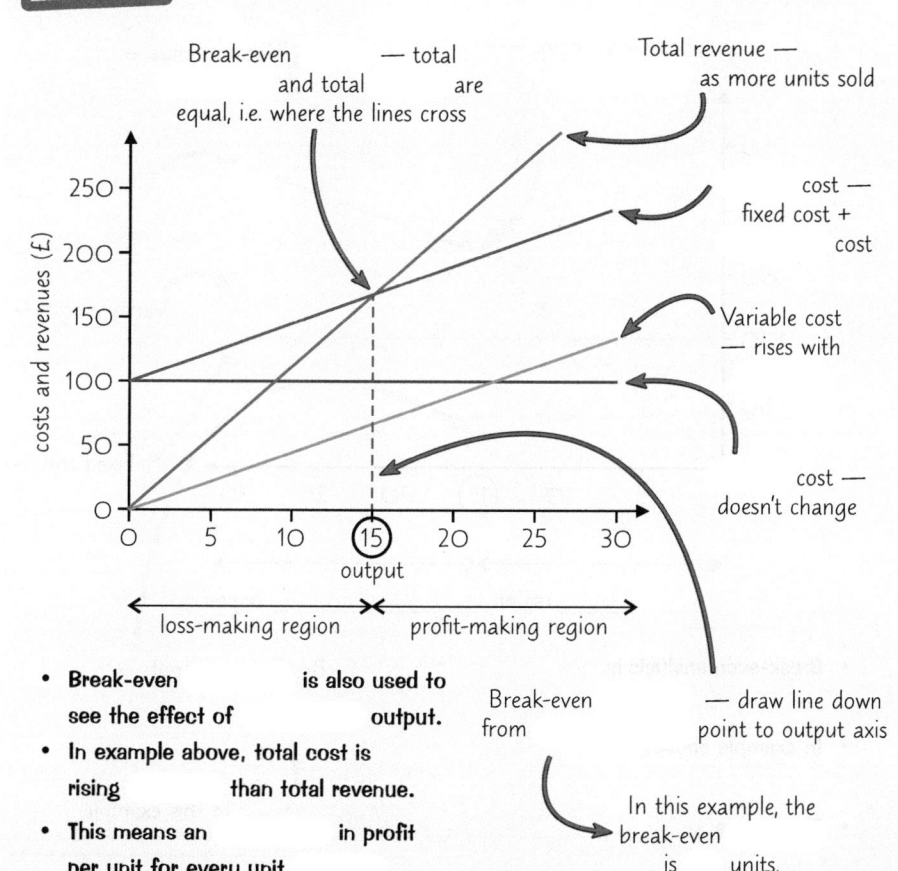

- Break-even _____ — total _____ and total _____ are equal, i.e. where the lines cross
- Total revenue — _____ as more units sold
- _____ cost — fixed cost + _____ cost
- Variable cost — rises with _____
- _____ cost — doesn't change
- Break-even _____ from _____ — draw line down _____ point to output axis
- In this example, the break-even _____ is _____ units.

(y-axis: costs and revenues (£), values 0, 50, 100, 150, 200, 250)
(x-axis: output, values 0, 5, 10, 15, 20, 25, 30)
loss-making region ← | → profit-making region

- Break-even _____ is also used to see the effect of _____ output.
- In example above, total cost is rising _____ than total revenue.
- This means an _____ in profit per unit for every unit _____.

Section 6 — Finance

Second Go:
..... / ..... / .....

Break-Even Analysis

Break-Even Output

BREAK-EVEN OUTPUT —

Selling more

Selling less

New businesses should

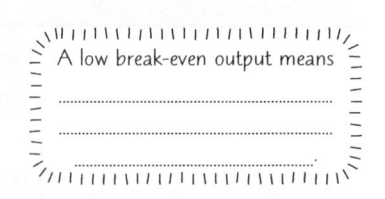

> A low break-even output means
> ....
> ....
> ....

Features of Break-Even Chart

EXAMPLE

Break-even point —

Total revenue —

Total cost —

Variable cost —

Fixed cost —

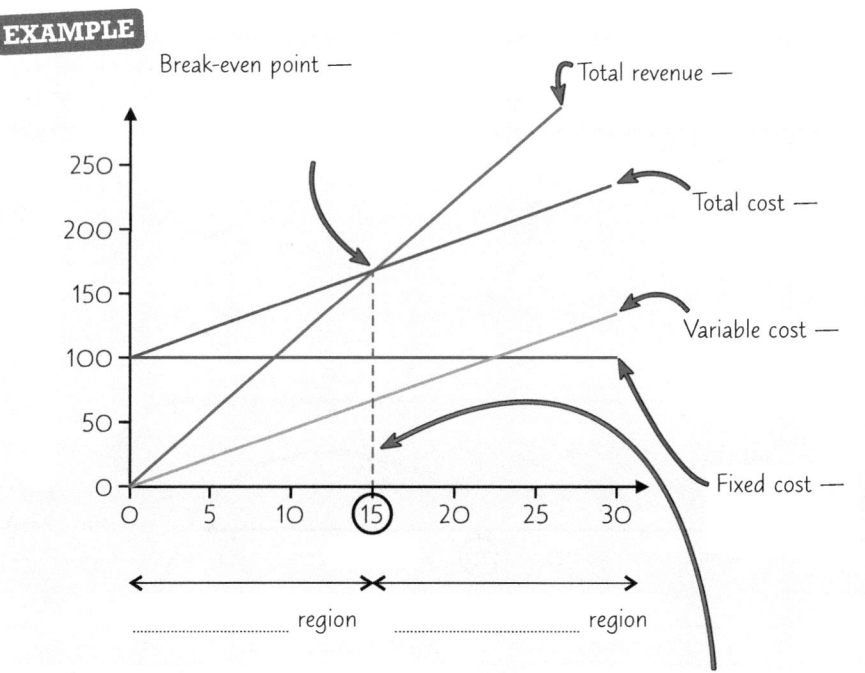

.... region .... region

Break-even output —

- **Break-even analysis is**

- **In example above,**

- **This means**

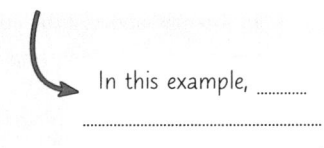

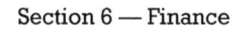

In this example, ...
....
....

Section 6 — Finance

More on Break-Even Analysis

First Go: ...../...../.....

Margin of Safety

MARGIN OF SAFETY — how much a business's .... can .... before a .... is made.

You can show the margin of safety on a .... chart.

EXAMPLE

margin of safety

.... output

Total revenue

Total cost

.... output

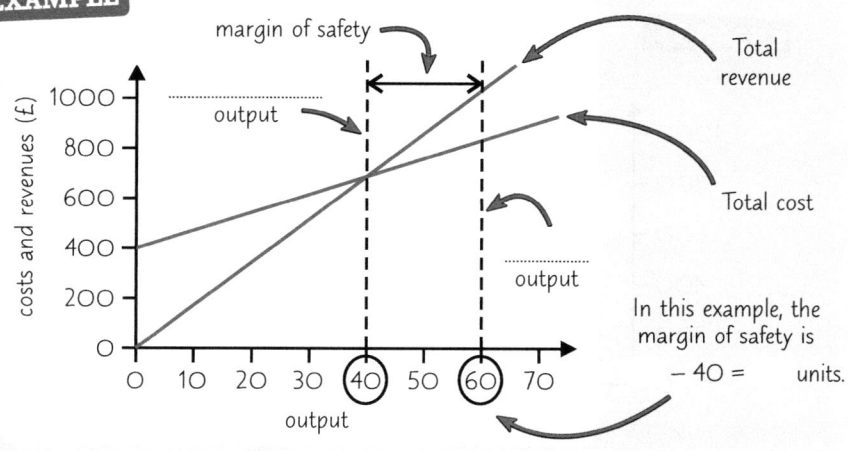

In this example, the margin of safety is .... − 40 = ... units.

(chart: costs and revenues (£) 0–1000 vs output 0–70, with 40 and 60 circled)

Five Advantages of Analysis

1. .... to work out.
2. It's .... to make. Immediate action can be taken to .... sales or .... costs.
3. Helps .... how changes in sales affect ....
4. Used to convince banks to give ....
5. Stops releasing products that are .... to sell in large ....

Five Disadvantages of Analysis

1. Assumes any .... of product can be sold at .... price.
2. Assumes all products are sold without ....
3. Wrong .... if data is ....
4. Complicated if more than .... product is involved.
5. Only shows what a firm .... to sell, not what it .... sell.

Section 6 — Finance

Second Go:
..... / ..... / .....

More on Break-Even Analysis

Margin of Safety

MARGIN OF SAFETY —

You can show

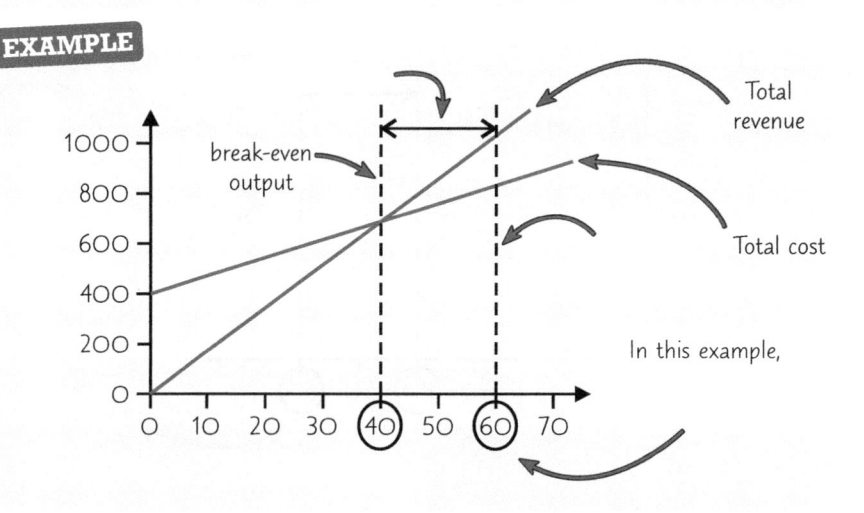

EXAMPLE

```
1000 |
 800 |          break-even
 600 |          output                    Total revenue
 400 |
 200 |                                    Total cost
   0 |_____
     0  10  20  30  (40)  50  (60)  70
```

In this example,

Five Advantages of Analysis

1.
2.
3. Helps predict
4.
5. Stops releasing

Five Disadvantages of Analysis

1. Assumes any quantity
2. Assumes all
3. Wrong results if
4. Complicated
5. Only shows

Section 6 — Finance

Cash Flow

First Go: ...../...../.....

Cash and Profit

CASH — the _____ that a business can _____ immediately.

- Cash is not the same as _____.
- _____ is the money a firm earns after _____ have been taken into account.
- A firm can make a _____ but run out of _____ if it uses it to invest in _____.

Cash Flow Forecasts

CASH FLOW FORECAST — _____ shows the cash expected to flow _____ and _____ the business over time.

- Used to show when a business won't have _____ cash.
- Can see when a _____ finance, e.g. an overdraft, may be _____.
- Should be watched carefully to monitor impact of _____ cash flows.

Opening balance = closing balance of _____ month

Closing balance = opening balance + _____

Net Cash Flow

CASH FLOW — the flow of money _____ and _____ a business.

When a firm _____ products there is a cash _____.

When a firm spends _____ (e.g. on wages or materials) there is a cash _____.

NET CASH FLOW — the difference between cash _____ and _____ over a period of _____.

A firm has a _____ cash flow when cash inflow is greater than outflow.

+ _____ firm will have no problem making _____

− _____ firm may be missing opportunities to _____

> A business can make an _____ even if it has a poor _____.

Cash Flow Forecast — Sweetie Chocs	Dec	Jan	Feb
Total receipts (cash inflow)	7000	800	5500
Total payments (cash outflow)	4500	4500	4000
Net cash flow (inflow − outflow)	2500	(3700)	1500
Opening balance (bank balance at start of month)	1000	3500	(200)
Closing balance (bank balance at end of month)	3500	(200)	1300

Net cash flow is _____ in January — outflow is greater than inflow.

Numbers in brackets are negative.

They will need _____ finance in January — knowing this in advance means they can _____.

Section 6 — Finance

Second Go: ..... /..... /.....

Cash Flow

Cash and Profit

CASH — the money that

- Cash is not
- Profit is

- A firm can

Cash Flow Forecasts

CASH FLOW FORECAST — shows the cash

- Used to show when

- Can see when

- Should be

Net Cash Flow

CASH FLOW —

When a firm sells

When a firm spends

NET CASH FLOW —

A firm has a positive

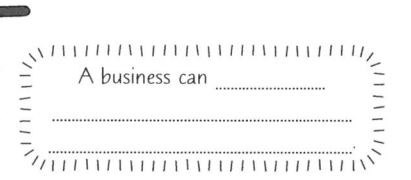

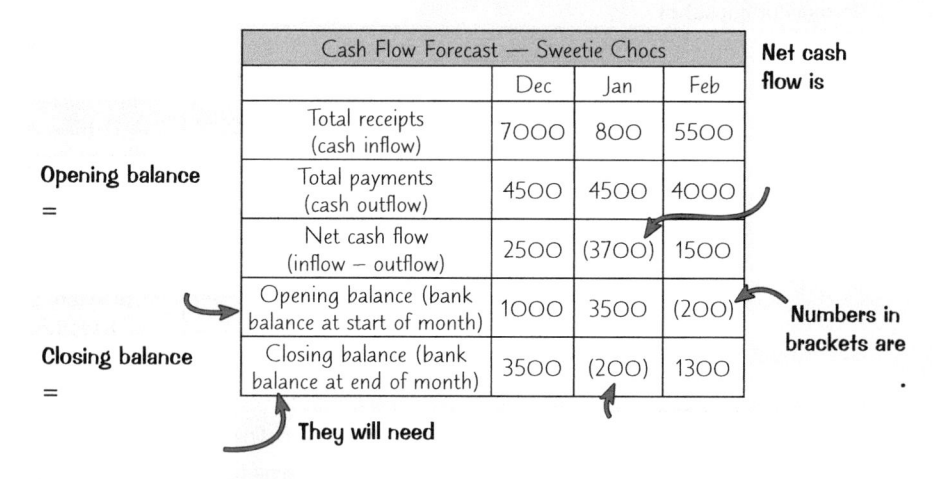

+
−

A business can ....

Cash Flow Forecast — Sweetie Chocs			
	Dec	Jan	Feb
Total receipts (cash inflow)	7000	800	5500
Total payments (cash outflow)	4500	4500	4000
Net cash flow (inflow − outflow)	2500	(3700)	1500
Opening balance (bank balance at start of month)	1000	3500	(200)
Closing balance (bank balance at end of month)	3500	(200)	1300

Net cash flow is

Opening balance =

Closing balance =

Numbers in brackets are

They will need

Section 6 — Finance

More on Cash Flow

First Go: ...../...../......

Three Effects of Poor Cash Flow

A poor cash flow means there isn't enough cash for .... expenses. Effects on a business include:

> Credit terms tell a customer how .... they have until they .... for a product.

1. staff not .... on .... and poor motivation
2. Creditors .... on time → may insist on .... terms or take .... offered by suppliers for .... → .... credit action .... payments
3. can't take advantage of ....

Three Reasons for Poor Cash Flow

1. Poor ....
   - Lack of .... from the .... for products.
   - Less .... coming in.

2. Overtrading
   - Firm takes on too many .... so buys lots of raw ....
   - Issue with .... means firm doesn't get .... from customers quickly enough to pay ....

3. Poor business ....
   - Firm brings out products in new .... that don't bring in as much .... as ....

Five Ways to Improve Cash Flow

1. Rescheduling ....
   - Give customers .... generous credit terms.
   - Negotiate better credit terms with ....

2. .... cash outflow
   - Firms may carry a .... of unsold products.
   - These could be .... instead of making ....

3. Arranging an ....

4. Finding .... finance sources

5. .... cash inflow

Section 6 — Finance

Second Go: ..... / ..... / .....

More on Cash Flow

Three Effects of Poor Cash Flow

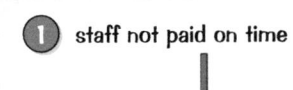

A poor cash flow means

Credit terms tell a customer ....

Effects on a business include:

1) staff not paid on time

2) creditors not paid on time

....
....

....
....

3) can't take advantage

Three Reasons for Poor Cash Flow

1) Poor sales
- Lack of

- Less

2) Overtrading
- Firm takes on

- Issue with

Five Ways to Improve Cash Flow

1) Rescheduling payments
- Give customers

- Negotiate

3) Poor business decisions
- Firm brings out

2) Reducing cash outflow
- Firms may

- These could be

4)

3)

5)

Section 6 — Finance

Mixed Practice Quizzes

Now you're into the flow of things, here are four more quizzes covering p.135-142. Mark each quiz yourself and work out your total score.

Quiz 1   Date: ...... / ...... / ......

1) What is cash flow?
2) True or false? The opening balance in a cash flow forecast is always greater than the closing balance from the previous month.
3) How can firms change customers' credit terms to improve cash flow?
4) What is plotted as a horizontal line on a break-even chart?
5) Describe how to calculate net cash flow.
6) True or false? A low break-even output means a firm has to sell less to make a profit.
7) Describe one effect that poor cash flow can have on the employees of a firm.
8) Give two assumptions that firms make when using a break-even analysis.
9) Give one potential disadvantage to a firm of having a positive cash flow.
10) List three advantages to a firm of doing a break-even analysis.

Total:

Quiz 2   Date: ...... / ...... / ......

1) Where is the break-even output found on a break-even chart?
2) Define 'cash' in terms of a business's finances.
3) What two values are added to find total cost on a break-even chart?
4) Give one way that a firm can reduce cash outflow.
5) What quantity is plotted on the horizontal axis of a break-even chart?
6) Give one source of cash inflow for a firm.
7) What are 'credit terms'?
8) True or false? Reducing costs can increase a firm's margin of safety.
9) List five disadvantages of a firm doing a break-even analysis.
10) Describe how to calculate the closing balance for a month in a cash flow forecast.

Total:

Mixed Practice Quizzes

Quiz 3   Date: ...... / ...... / ......

1) How is the profit per unit affected if the total cost is rising more slowly than the total revenue on a break-even chart?
2) What two values must be equal at the break-even point?
3) Give one benefit to a firm of having a positive cash flow.
4) List three reasons for poor cash flow.
5) What is the difference between cash and profit?
6) What is meant by 'margin of safety'?
7)* In January, a firm has cash inflows of £7000 and cash outflows of £5600. Calculate the net cash flow.
8) True or false? A firm makes a profit when it sells less than its break-even output.
9) What are the consequences to a firm of not paying creditors on time?
10) What does a cash flow forecast show?

Total:

Quiz 4   Date: ...... / ...... / ......

1) Define 'break-even output'.
2) What can a business use to show when it might run out of cash?
3) What can make break-even analysis more complicated for a firm?
4) List three effects of poor cash flow on a firm.
5)* One month, a firm has an opening balance of £350. Their net cash flow for the month is −£150. What is their closing balance for the month?
6) Give two examples of cash outflows in a business.
7) What do numbers in brackets represent in a cash flow forecast?
8) True or false? When a firm lowers prices, it must sell more to break even.
9) List five ways to improve cash flow.
10) Describe how the margin of safety is found on a break-even chart.

Total:

145

Income Statements

First Go: ...../...../......

Three Parts to Income Statements

INCOME STATEMENT — statement that shows how _____ has _____ over time.

① The _____ account — records _____ or _____ over a period of time.
- Revenue — the _____ of all products _____.
- Cost of sales — how _____ the products cost _____ to _____ (the _____ costs).

cost of sales = (_____ stock + purchases) – _____ stock

_____ = revenue – cost of sales

② The _____ and _____ account — records indirect costs of running the business.
- Covers the cost of _____ (amount of value an asset has lost).
- Money left after indirect costs (expenses) is the _____.
- After _____ paid (or received) is included, _____ is left over.

③ The _____ account — records where the _____ has gone.

Income Statement
Superb Sofas Ltd.
Year ending 31st March 2024

means numbers shown are in the thousands — £000 £000

Revenue		250
Cost of sales:		
Opening stock	5	
Purchases	45	
	50	
Minus closing stock	(4)	
Cost of sales =		(46)
Gross profit =		204

Minus expenses		
Wages and salaries	108	
Rents and rates	16	
Office expenses	10	
Advertising	11	
Depreciation	9	
Other expenses	2	
Expenses =		(156)
Operating profit =		48
Interest payable		(2)
Profit before tax (Net profit)		46

Taxation	(9)
Dividends	(18)
Retained profit	19

Business Performance from Income Statement Values

_____ profit — if it is low then ways of _____ revenue or _____ costs should be explored to make gross profit _____.

_____ profit — weak area if it is significantly _____ than _____ profit. If it is too low, banks will be _____ to _____.

_____ profit — shows _____ of a firm. A larger _____ profit shows the business has potential to get _____.

Section 6 — Finance

Income Statements

Three Parts to Income Statements

INCOME STATEMENT —

① The trading account —

- Revenue —

- Cost of sales — how much
  (the direct costs).

$$\text{cost of sales} = (\qquad + \qquad) - $$

gross profit =   −

② The profit and loss account —

- Covers the cost of

- Money left after

- After interest paid

③ The appropriation account —

	Income Statement Superb Sofas Ltd. Year ending 31st March 2024 means numbers shown are in the thousands → £000	£000
Revenue		250
Cost of sales:		
Opening stock	5	
Purchases	45	
	50	
Minus closing stock	(4)	
Cost of sales =		(46)
Gross profit =		204
Minus expenses		
Wages and salaries	108	
Rents and rates	16	
Office expenses	10	
Advertising	11	
Depreciation	9	
Other expenses	2	
Expenses =		(156)
Operating profit =		48
Interest payable		(2)
Profit before tax (Net profit)		46
Taxation		(9)
Dividends		(18)
Retained profit		19

Business Performance from Income Statement Values

Gross profit — if it is low then

Operating profit — weak area if it is

Retained profit — shows

Section 6 — Finance

Profit Margins

First Go: ..... / ..... / .....

Gross Profit Margin

GROSS PROFIT MARGIN — the fraction of every .... spent by .... that doesn't go directly towards ....

$$\text{gross profit margin} = \frac{\rule{2cm}{0.4pt}}{\rule{2cm}{0.4pt}} \times 100$$

Can be improved by:
- ↑ increasing ....
- ↓ reducing ....

Higher gross profit margin is .... , but what counts as a 'good' profit margin depends on the ....

> E.g. supermarkets have .... gross profit margins because they keep .... to compete, but can still make .... as they sell in ....

Net Profit Margin

NET PROFIT MARGIN — the .... of every pound spent by .... that the business ....

$$\text{net profit margin} = \frac{\rule{2cm}{0.4pt}}{\rule{2cm}{0.4pt}} \times 100$$

Like for .... , ... net profit margin is better, but what counts as a 'good' margin depends on the ....

> Net profit margin can .... as a firm .... and has more .... (e.g. more .... , more spent on .... or ....).

EXAMPLE

In one year, Polly's Paper made a gross profit of £72 000 from a revenue of £180 000. Calculate the gross profit margin.

gross profit margin

$$= \frac{\rule{1.5cm}{0.4pt}}{\rule{1.5cm}{0.4pt}} \times 100$$

$$= \frac{\rule{1.5cm}{0.4pt}}{\rule{1.5cm}{0.4pt}} \times 100$$

$$= \rule{1cm}{0.4pt} \times \rule{1cm}{0.4pt} = \rule{1cm}{0.4pt} \%$$

In the same year, Polly's Paper had operating expenses of £42 000 and paid £3000 of interest on loans. Calculate the net profit margin.

net profit = ... − (operating expenses + interest)

$$= \rule{1cm}{0.4pt} - (\rule{1cm}{0.4pt} + \rule{1cm}{0.4pt})$$

$$= \rule{1cm}{0.4pt} - \rule{1cm}{0.4pt}$$

$$= £\rule{1cm}{0.4pt}$$

net profit margin

$$= \frac{\rule{1.5cm}{0.4pt}}{\rule{1.5cm}{0.4pt}} \times 100$$

$$= \frac{\rule{1.5cm}{0.4pt}}{\rule{1.5cm}{0.4pt}} \times 100$$

$$= \rule{1cm}{0.4pt} \times 100 = \rule{1cm}{0.4pt} \%$$

Section 6 — Finance

Second Go:
..... / ..... / .....

Profit Margins

Gross Profit Margin

GROSS PROFIT MARGIN —

gross profit margin =

Can be improved by:
↑
↓

Higher is ...., but what counts as a .... depends on the ....

E.g. supermarkets have ....
....
....

EXAMPLE

In one year, Polly's Paper made a gross profit of £72 000 from a revenue of £180 000. Calculate the gross profit margin.

gross profit margin

=

=

= =

In the same year, Polly's Paper had operating expenses of £42 000 and paid £3000 of interest on loans. Calculate the net profit margin.

net profit
=
=
= =

net profit margin

=

= 15%

Net Profit Margin

NET PROFIT MARGIN —

net profit margin =

Like for gross profit margin,

Net profit margin can .... as a firm ....
....
....

Section 6 — Finance

Statements of Financial Position

First Go: ..... / ..... / .....

Fixed Assets

STATEMENT OF FINANCIAL POSITION — shows .... a business got its .... from and what's .... with it.

The .... of a statement of financial position shows what has .... with the money.

A business uses some .... to buy ....
The total figure shown is what they're .... on the .... of the statement.

Current Assets

Current assets .... — listed from .... to .... liquid.
- **Stock** — .... and finished products that have not been ....
- **Debtors** — sold products that haven't been paid for by .... yet.
- **Cash** — .... that hasn't been .... yet.

Current Liabilities

.... that have to be made within a .... of the date on the statement.
- **Creditors** — .... that the firm owes to ....
- **Corporation tax** — payable to .... out of the year's profit.

Net Assets

NET CURRENT ASSETS — money available for .... operations.
Also known as ....

Can be worked out by subtracting the current .... from the current ....

EXAMPLE

Statement of Financial Position
Polly's Pizza Ltd., 31st March 2024

	£000	£000
Fixed assets		
Premises		60
Machinery		20
Vehicles		30
		110
Current assets		
Stock	5	
Debtors	15	
Cash	7	
	27	
Current liabilities		
Creditors	(21)	
Corporation tax	(2)	
	(23)	
Net current assets		4
Net assets		114
Financed by		
Shareholders' funds		
Share capital		65
Retained profit		20
Long-term liabilities		
Bank loan		21
Mortgage		8
Capital employed		114

NET ASSETS — what the business is .... (if it .... all its assets).
Can be worked out by adding .... assets to .... assets.

Section 6 — Finance

Statements of Financial Position

Second Go: ..../..../.....

Fixed Assets

STATEMENT OF FINANCIAL POSITION —

The first part of ....

A business uses

The total figure shown is

EXAMPLE

```
Statement of Financial Position
Polly's Pizza Ltd., 31st March 2024
                           £000    £000
Fixed assets
  Premises                          60
  Machinery                         20
  Vehicles                          30
                                   110
Current assets
  Stock                     5
  Debtors                  15
  Cash                      7
                           27
Current liabilities
  Creditors              (21)
  Corporation tax         (2)
                         (23)
Net current assets                   4
Net assets                         114

Financed by
Shareholders' funds
  Share capital                     65
  Retained profit                   20
Long-term liabilities
  Bank loan                         21
  Mortgage                           8
Capital employed                   114
```

Current Assets

Current assets —

- Stock —

- Debtors —

- Cash —

Current Liabilities

Payments that have to be

- Creditors —

- Corporation tax —

Net Assets

NET CURRENT ASSETS — money available

Also known as
Can be worked out by

NET ASSETS —

Can be worked out by

Section 6 — Finance

More on Statements of Financial Position

First Go: ...../...../......

Two Parts to Shareholders' Funds

The .... of a statement of financial position is where all the money ....

1) Share capital
- .... put into the business when .... were originally issued.
- Not the same as what shares are ....
- Firms can raise new .... by issuing ....

Can be done through a ...., where existing .... are offered new shares at .... prices.

EXAMPLE

Financed by	
Shareholders' funds	
Share capital	65
Retained profit	20
Long-term liabilities	
Bank loan	21
Mortgage	8
Capital employed	114

2) Retained profits and ....
- Profit the firm has made .... that it has kept instead of paying out ....
- Profit is .... to finance .... and .... to protect against ....
- Falls under the shareholders' funds as .... are really their money — it's just been .... the firm.

Long-Term Liabilities

- Firms also get .... from sources other than ....
- Any .... that will take .... a year to .... are long-term liabilities.

Capital Employed

The .... accounts for all the firm's .... of money.

.... capital employed = ... funds + ... liabilities

Capital employed is .... net assets.

Money the firm got (capital employed) must be .... what the firm .... with that money (net assets).

Section 6 — Finance

Second Go: ..../..../.... More on Statements of Financial Position

Two Parts to Shareholders' Funds

The second part of ....

EXAMPLE

Financed by	
Shareholders' funds	
Share capital	65
Retained profit	20
Long-term liabilities	
Bank loan	21
Mortgage	8
Capital employed	114

1) Share capital
- Money put
- Not the same as
- Firms can

Can be done through ....

2) Retained profits and reserves
- Profit the firm has
- Profit is
- Falls under

Long-Term Liabilities

- Firms also
- Any debts

Capital Employed

The capital employed

capital employed =   +

Capital employed is

Money the ....
must be equal to ....

Section 6 — Finance

Analysis of Financial Statements

First Go: ..... / ..... / .....

Uses of Statements of Financial Position

A firm can use its _____ and _____ to help make business decisions.

Statements of financial position can:

- be used to _____ a firm's _____ at a point in time.
- show sources of _____.
- be used to work out _____ and _____.

Three Trends Over Time

Statements of financial position can be _____ over a number of _____.

Three things to compare are:

1. Fixed assets — a quick _____ implies business has _____.
2. _____ profits — increase _____ suggests an _____ in profits.
3. Liabilities — amount and _____ show how _____ a firm is.

Five Stakeholders Interested in Financial Analysis

	Stakeholder	Why they assess the statement
1	Existing shareholders	To see if _____ are making _____ decisions.
2	Potential shareholders or _____	May consider _____ if the business is making lots of _____.
3	_____	They may get a _____ if the business is _____.
4	The government	To see how much _____ a business _____.
5	_____	Higher _____ means firm is _____ to pay bills on time.

Comparing Financial Statements of Competitors

- Income statements can be used to compare _____, expenses and _____.
- Statements of financial position can compare each firm's _____ and their _____.
- Some firms are _____ to compare as they can _____ in different ways. Direct comparison can be done by calculating _____ and _____ margins.

Section 6 — Finance

Analysis of Financial Statements

Second Go: ..... / ..... / .....

Uses of Statements of Financial Position

Statements of financial position can:
- be used to

- show
- be used to

A firm can use ....

Three Trends Over Time

Statements of financial position can be

Three things to compare are:

1 Fixed assets —

2 Retained profits —

3 Liabilities —

Five Stakeholders Interested in Financial Analysis

Stakeholder	Why they assess the statement
1 Existing shareholders	To see if
2	May consider
3 Employees	They may get
4	
5 Suppliers	Higher liquidity means

Comparing Financial Statements of Competitors

- Income statements can be

- Statements of financial position can

- Some firms are hard to compare as

Section 6 — Finance

Mixed Practice Quizzes

Congratulations — you've made it to the final set of quizzes in the book. See what you can recall from p.145-154, then mark your answers and add up your scores.

Quiz 1   Date: ...... / ...... / ......

1) What is the formula to calculate cost of sales?
2) What is meant by 'share capital' on a statement of financial position?
3) What does a quick increase in fixed assets indicate a business has done?
4) What is the expression $\frac{\text{net profit}}{\text{revenue}} \times 100$ used to calculate?
5) True or false? The first part of a statement of financial position shows where a firm's money has come from.
6) List the three accounts that an income statement is broken up into.
7) What is the money left after expenses called in an income statement?
8) List three current assets a firm may have, from least to most liquid.
9) What is meant by 'net profit margin'?
10) Why might suppliers be interested in a firm's financial analysis?

Total:

Quiz 2   Date: ...... / ...... / ......

1)* Find the gross profit margin if gross profit = £2m and revenue = £8m.
2) What does a statement of financial position show?
3) Name the two parts of a statement of financial position that are added together to calculate capital employed.
4) What does the trading account on an income statement record?
5) True or false? Increasing a product's price reduces its gross profit margin.
6) How does a low operating profit affect a firm's ability to attract investors?
7) List five stakeholders that are interested in the financial analysis of a firm.
8) How can the net current assets of a firm be calculated?
9) What is meant by 'depreciation' on an income statement?
10) What is recorded in the appropriation account of an income statement?

Total:

Section 6 — Finance

Mixed Practice Quizzes

Quiz 3 Date: ...... / ...... / ......

1) Explain the difference between long-term liabilities and current liabilities.
2) What is meant by 'net assets'?
3)* Find the net profit margin if net profit = £1.2m and revenue = £6m.
4) Which stakeholder is interested in how much tax a business owes?
5) What does an income statement show?
6) True or false? The total of a firm's fixed assets is what the firm is worth on the date of the statement.
7) What is meant by 'net current assets' on a statement of financial position?
8) State two ways a firm could improve the gross profit margin on a product.
9) What is the expression 'revenue − cost of sales' used to calculate?
10) Why might net profit margin decrease as a firm grows?

Total:

Quiz 4 Date: ...... / ...... / ......

1) Give two examples of current liabilities a firm may have.
2) What formula is used to calculate gross profit margin?
3) Why do retained profits and reserves fall underneath shareholders' funds in a statement of financial position?
4) What is meant by 'gross profit margin'?
5) True or false? Capital employed is never equal to net assets.
6) Why might potential shareholders and lenders be interested in a firm's financial analysis?
7) Which account on an income statement records the indirect costs of running a business?
8) List three things that a statement of financial position can be used for.
9) What does a larger retained profit suggest about a firm's profits?
10) In a statement of financial position, what is meant by 'stock'?

Total:

Section 6 — Finance

Answers

Section 1 — Business in the Real World

Pages 29-30

Quiz 1
Q6　average unit cost
　　= total cost ÷ output
　　= £10 000 ÷ 50
　　= £200

Quiz 2
Q7　profit = revenue − cost
　　= £44 000 − £32 000
　　= £12 000

Quiz 3
Q9　revenue
　　= quantity sold × price
　　= 500 × £200
　　= £100 000

Quiz 4
Q3　total cost
　　= total fixed cost + total variable cost
　　= £6000 + £7500
　　= £13 500

Section 6 — Finance

Pages 133-134

Quiz 1
Q2　average annual profit
　　$= \dfrac{\text{total profit}}{\text{number of years}}$
　　$= \dfrac{£1\,200\,000}{4}$
　　= £300 000

Q6　ARR
　　$= \dfrac{\text{average annual profit}}{\text{cost of investment}} \times 100$
　　$= \dfrac{£400\,000}{£1\,000\,000} \times 100$
　　= 40%

Quiz 2
Q2　average annual profit
　　$= \dfrac{\text{total profit}}{\text{number of years}}$
　　$= \dfrac{£2\,400\,000}{6}$
　　= £400 000

Quiz 3
Q3　ARR
　　$= \dfrac{\text{average annual profit}}{\text{cost of investment}} \times 100$
　　$= \dfrac{£500\,000}{£5\,000\,000} \times 100$
　　= 10%

Quiz 4
Q1　average annual profit
　　$= \dfrac{\text{total profit}}{\text{number of years}}$
　　$= \dfrac{£900\,000}{3}$
　　= £300 000

Q9　ARR
　　$= \dfrac{\text{average annual profit}}{\text{cost of investment}} \times 100$
　　$= \dfrac{£2\,000\,000}{£4\,000\,000} \times 100$
　　= 50%

Answers

Pages 143-144

Quiz 3
Q7 net cash flow
= cash inflows − cash outflows
= £7000 − £5600
= £1400

Quiz 4
Q5 closing balance
= opening balance + net cash flow
= £350 + (− £150)
= £200

Pages 155-156

Quiz 2
Q1 gross profit margin
$$= \frac{\text{gross profit}}{\text{revenue}} \times 100$$
$$= \frac{£2\,000\,000}{£8\,000\,000} \times 100$$
$$= 25\%$$

Quiz 3
Q3 net profit margin
$$= \frac{\text{net profit}}{\text{revenue}} \times 100$$
$$= \frac{£1\,200\,000}{£6\,000\,000} \times 100$$
$$= 20\%$$